The
Pursuit
of
Purpose

A 40-year journey of
a Dutch Flower Farmer
in America

Lane DeVries

All photographs courtesy of Lane DeVries, except for 1986 aerial picture, creator unknown on page 36, photograph of George Heublein from Bloembollencutuur magazine August 25th 1988 on page 40, Frank Riggs picture from Times Standard October 16th 1992 on page 58, 1998 aerial by Sy Beatte on page 61, Arcata Eye frontpage article February 11th 1997 on page 72, X-rays from Mad River Hospital July 17th 2007 on page 91, picture of greenhouse from Humboldt Botanical Society on page 133, front cover of SAF's Floral Management magazine on page 153, picture of devastation in Paradise from Daily Mail November 16th 2018 on page 185, satellite picture of Jordan River on page 216.

Edited by Dennis Kouba
Cover and interior formatting by KUHN Design Group | kuhndesigngroup.com

The Pursuit of Purpose: A 40-Year Journey of a Dutch Flower Farmer in America
© 2025 by Lane DeVries

Printed in the United States of America

ISBN: 979-8-9935676-0-0 (paperback)
ISBN: 979-8-9935676-2-4 (hardcover)
ISBN: 979-8-9935676-1-7 (eBook)

First Edition

Library of Congress Control Number: 2025923209

For more information, please visit:
www.lanedevries.com

PRAISE FOR *THE PURSUIT OF PURPOSE*

This is far more than a business memoir, it's a moving and masterfully told story about legacy, leadership, and the quiet strength that comes from living a life of purpose. With authenticity and grace, Lane Devries shares a 40-year journey that mirrors the very nature of the flowers he grew, rooted deeply, shaped by the seasons, and made beautiful through resilience.

From humble beginnings to building the nation's largest flower farm, this book captures not only the evolution of an industry, but the transformation of a life grounded in values, faith, and meaning. Every page reveals insights that extend well beyond agriculture, touching on what it truly means to build something that matters and to lead with heart.

If you're looking for inspiration, wisdom, and a genuine reminder that purpose often grows through adversity, you'll find it here.

> **Barry Gottlieb,** Author of Brilliant on the Basics, Every Day is a Gift, TGIT, Horizons of Growth, and This Old Dog Can Teach You New Tricks...

If you've ever wondered how great companies endure, this candid and moving story from the founder of Sun Valley Floral Farms shows the formula for success: relentless improvement, radical transparency, and a people-first culture that holds in every storm. DeVries turns numerous personal challenges and business setbacks into a practical playbook for resilience—ten principles you can use tomorrow to build something that lasts by anchoring in purpose.

> **Dr. Charles R. (Charlie) Hall,** Professor & Ellison Chair in International Floriculture, Texas A&M University

In his highly personal memoir, Lane weaves lessons of faith into his floral story. Having devoted more than four decades to flower farming, he maintains an optimism, sense of calling, and an unwavering passion for growing flowers that readers will find inspiring.

> **Debra Prinzing,** Author and founder of the Slow Flowers Movement

"In a country of instant 'fame and fortune,' a Dutch flower farmer had a dream, a long, well thought out dream that he put into reality with a plan, perseverance, commitment and very hard work. This book journals the how-to's for flower lovers and business students alike. A guide to success and branding in a world with hollow brands. This is the real story, filled with wisdom and spirituality by one of the most passionate and humble flower growers I have had the pleasure of working with for a long time." A success story, filled with lessons.

Rene van Rems, AIFD, Dutch master designer, presenter and author

This book is Enthralling from the First Paragraph… and it's an incredible testament to DeVries's Perseverance in the face of difficulties and challenges… this book provides Great Insights to Pursuing Your Own Purpose…with faith and love! "

J Schwanke, Host of "J Schwanke's Life in Bloom" on PBS and Create TV

"As someone who has witnessed Lane DeVries' extraordinary journey firsthand and partnered with Sun Valley to bring millions of flowers to customers across America, I can say there is no one better equipped to tell the true story of purpose, perseverance, and innovation in our industry. The Pursuit of Purpose is not just a memoir, it's a masterclass in leadership, resilience, and the kind of values that every entrepreneur, dreamer, and business leader should aspire to embrace."

Jim McCann, Founder and chairman of 1-800-flowers

I dedicate this book to my wife, Kathryn, who stood by me through the good times, and especially when things got tough.

CONTENTS

Adhere to your purpose and you will soon feel as well as you ever did. On the contrary, if you falter, and give up, you will lose the power of keeping any resolution and will regret it all your life.

Always bear in mind that your own resolution to success is more important than any other thing. In the end it's not the years in your life that count. It's the life in your years.

ABRAHAM LINCOLN

FOREWORD

This book, authored by Lane DeVries, whom I knew when we lived in Humboldt County, California, is a remarkable piece of literature. This is a book that should be read by everyone, but especially high school and college students, since it provides very thoughtful ideas for having a good and successful life. The book presents a history of how Lane's company, Sun Valley Floral, was created and grew to impressive success even when faced with significant competition and troublesome government decisions. Anyone interested in developing a business should read this book and learn about the issues that are so important for success as a businessperson.

The first part of the book tells how Lane DeVries moved to California from Holland, part of the Netherlands, where his family had been growing flowers over several generations. The expansion of Lane's business was amazing. As he writes, "…real growth doesn't come from shortcuts. It comes from relationships built on trust, and from doing the hard work, quietly, consistently, and with purpose." You will learn that Sun Valley Floral provided leadership on many important issues such as promoting Women's Day.

DeVries love of religion and his efforts to educate others about Christianity started when he took a trip to Israel. He also began to give sermons to churches close to Sun Valley Floral. As Lane writes, religion " eventually became a treasured chapter of my life, one filled with meaning, growth, and purpose.

One of the important points DeVries makes frequently in his book is that you need a set of guidelines not only for your business, but also your life. DeVries lists ten guidelines for business and life.

Read this book. It will influence your future.

Rollin C. Richmond
President Emeritus of Cal Polytech University Humboldt

PROLOGUE

W hen the journey of our business, Sun Valley Floral Farms, came to an end, it marked the close of a remarkable chapter, one that had shaped the better part of my life for more than 40 years. While there was a natural sense of melancholy, it was soon joined by a deep gratitude for all that we had built. Sun Valley wasn't just a company, it was a community, a calling, and a way of life. The experience touched countless lives, leaving a profound impact not only on the team members within our organization, but also on many throughout the floral industry, both in the United States and abroad.

Over the years, numerous people have encouraged me to write this book to capture and commemorate the fascinating ride I've been blessed to experience over the past four decades.

This story begins in the 1980s and takes the reader on a remarkable journey spanning 40 years, years marked by blessings and adventure, soaring highs and humbling hardships. But at its heart, this is a story about the relentless pursuit of purpose.

That pursuit of purpose is the thread that weaves through the chapters, shaping what Sun Valley became and what so many in the flower industry remember it for. There's something deeply meaningful about a 40-year span. Moses, for example, spent his first 40 years in Egypt among his fellow Israelites in captivity, followed by 40 years tending sheep on his father-in-law's land. It was then that God revealed his true purpose, to lead his people out of Egypt, and the final 40 years of his life were spent in the desert fulfilling that calling.

The weight of those 40-year periods is not lost here. It's one of the book's central undercurrents: the idea that the pursuit of purpose doesn't begin or end, it evolves, day by day, year by year, over the decades.

Although my own story began in the mid-1980s, flower cultivation in the U.S. had already been flourishing for nearly 150 years prior. It's a rich and fascinating history that laid the foundation for the industry I would eventually enter. Flower growing in America began in the late 1800s, primarily near major cities such as New York, Philadelphia, and Chicago. With the arrival of the transcontinental railroad, fresh-cut flowers could suddenly travel great distances, allowing growers to reach customers far beyond their local markets.

As the decades passed, California and Colorado emerged as major production centers. By the 1970s, Colorado had become known as the Carnation Capital of the World. Denver Wholesale Florists, a cooperative of 70 growers, was shipping over 100 million carnation stems a year, an astonishing figure that spoke to both the scale and passion behind the business.

California, however, fast became the epicenter of flower farming in the United States. From the fields and greenhouses north of San Diego to the growers in the San Francisco Bay Area stretching down to Salinas, flower production boomed. It was here that names such as Kitayama, Shibata, Vanni, Obertello, Cozzolino, Yamaguchi, Nakashima, Kohara, and Kubota made their mark. After the Second World War, more than 80 flower shippers were operating in the Bay Area alone. When I entered the scene in the 1980s, I remember names like Bill Suyeyasu, Bob Gilmore, Stonehurst, Cut Flower Exchange, and GR Brown, names that, today, exist only in memory.

The early pioneers of the flower industry were largely of Italian and Japanese descent. After World War II a wave of Dutch flower farmers began settling in California, particularly in Carpinteria, south of Santa Barbara. Around the same time, Dutch bulb growers began making a home in the Pacific Northwest, near Mt. Vernon and Puyallup, Washington.

It was against this backdrop that I arrived in the United States from Holland, a young man with $160 in his pocket and a heart full of ambition. I didn't know it then, but I was stepping into a legacy, a lineage of growers and dreamers, innovators and risk-takers. Over the years, through hard work, good fortune, and the support of many remarkable people, we would go on to build a company that became the largest flower farm in the country. It was not an easy road, but it was a path deeply rooted in the rich soil of American flower farming history. And I am proud to have played a part in carrying that tradition forward.

The passing of the Andean Trade Preference Act in 1991 marked a turning point in the flower industry, triggering a dramatic shift in production. Domestic flower farmers saw their market share begin to erode, unable to compete with the influx of lower-priced imports.

Over the past 40 years of flower farming in California, I've had a front-row seat to this transformation. When I first arrived in the U.S. in my twenties, domestically grown flowers accounted for about 70% of the market. Today, that number has dropped to less than 20%.

Many of the great names and companies I admired when I first came to this country, pillars of the industry who inspired and influenced my own journey, are no longer around. And now, with a heavy heart, I must acknowledge that Sun Valley has joined that long list of once-thriving companies that ultimately succumbed to mounting economic pressures.

Ironically, Sun Valley's rise began in the very decade that marked the decline of much of the domestic flower industry. During the 1990s, while carnation growers were closing their doors, soon followed by rose and chrysanthemum growers, Sun Valley was growing faster than ever. In those early years, our focus on bulb flowers gave us a unique advantage; our product mix was relatively insulated from the imported flowers coming into the market.

All this eventually changed, as I'll describe in this book.

In the end, though, the floral industry has been good to me. I'm deeply grateful for the countless blessings my Heavenly Father has poured into my life throughout this journey.

What follows in these pages is more than a story about flowers. It's a story about purpose, perseverance, and the deeper meaning of life. Along the way, I've included illustrations of guiding principles, lessons established in the soil of hard work, failure, resilience, and grace. These principles aren't limited to agriculture or business. They're universal, and I believe they can speak to anyone navigating change, building something from the ground up, or simply trying to live a life of meaning and integrity and purpose.

The discerning reader will also notice an underlying faith journey woven throughout this story. It takes center stage a little over midway in the book in the chapters, *Purpose Journey* and *A New Beginning*. In the *Guiding Principles* section there are references, in the decisions made and the values upheld. The book describes quiet moments of surrender and trust. My hope is that these reflections will resonate with those who are open to receiving, encouraging them in their own walk, whatever path they may be on.

Whether you're a flower person, an entrepreneur, a dreamer, a believer, or simply someone curious about the story I am about to tell, I invite you to read on. This is the story of a life shaped by soil and Spirit, and I'm honored to share it with you.

CHAPTER 1

HOLLAND BEGINNINGS

Enthusiasm is the yeast that makes your hopes shine to the stars.
Enthusiasm is the sparkle in your eyes, the swing in your step. The
grip in your hand; the irresistible surge of will and energy to execute.

HENRY FORD

T he story starts in Holland. I was the third child in a family of four, with an older brother, an older sister, and a baby sister. I can proudly say that I am a fourth-generation flower farmer, a legacy that runs deep in our family's veins. Our farm was nestled in a region known for its small soil-grown tulip farms, Beverwijk-Heemskerk, the heartland of the "Coastulips." It was a place where generations of hard work and respect for the land were simply part of life.

I grew up surrounded by a wonderful, close-knit family. My mom was very caring, and my dad was a hard-working small flower farmer.

Dad's days were spent tending to tulips and daffodils in the winter green-houses, growing summer flowers from seed in the field , and potted plants in the greenhouse in summer. His passion for growing things wasn't just a job; it was who he was. On top of running the farm, he also operated a wholesale flower business, loading up his van full of flowers and driving to Haarlem and Amsterdam three times a week. Retail florists would buy directly from his truck, and those like him earned the nickname "Flying Dutchmen." Especially after the Second World War, this became a common way to bring flowers to market all across Holland and Western Europe, a tradition rooted in grit, creativity, and daring.

A portion of our flowers were sold through the local flower auction in Beverwijk, which was still operating in the 1980s. But most were sold along dad's flower route, face-to-face with loyal customers who knew the quality of what he grew. The auction itself was small, just two simple buildings, one for vegetables and one for flowers. It had its own unique rhythm: it was the only auction in Holland that sold flowers in the afternoon. Everywhere else, the auctions started at 6:00 a.m.

When the market was hot, big exporters such as Zurel and Fleura would scramble to Beverwijk to scoop up whatever they hadn't secured earlier that morning. But on slow days, when the morning auctions had satisfied all their demand, Beverwijk could feel empty, and the prices would tumble. There was a certain drama to it all, an unpredictability that shaped our daily lives.

My mom stayed at home, raising us kids and helping with the business whenever needed. She had a quiet but powerful way of encouraging us to dream bigger and to continue learning beyond high school. My brother and youngest sister both pursued law, and my brother would eventually serve as an appeals court judge. My older sister built a career in the medical field.

I was the only one who kept the flame alive, the only one who answered the call to continue our family's farming tradition. After graduating from horticultural college, I came back to work full-time on the farm. Those were formative years, years during which I really learned what it meant to work the land and build something with your own two hands.

As my father focused more on his flower route, I took charge of the farm. Our sales climbed steadily, especially with summer crops, and we continued growing our tulips and daffodils through the winter months.

But change was coming, whether we were ready or not. Our farm sat on land owned by a church foundation, and as the city of Beverwijk grew, the foundation decided to sell the land for residential development. They made us an offer to vacate, and with heavy hearts, we accepted. While we searched for a new farm, a friend of mine, who grew lilies in the neighboring town of Heemskerk, offered me a job. It was a lifeline. I had never grown lilies before, but I was eager to learn. There was something exciting about stepping into the unknown. At that time, they were growing mostly Asiatic varieties such as Enchantment, Connecticut King, Harmony, and Firecracker. Some Speciosum lilies like Rubrum were still around, too, though those would fade from production in the years ahead. Oriental lilies were just beginning to make their appearance. I remember working with a variety called "Journey's End," one of the very first Orientals, with its down-facing flowers.

And then there was "Stargazer." I'll never forget the buzz of excitement surrounding it, the first Oriental lily with upward-facing blooms! It felt like we were witnessing a revolution in the lily world. Back then, Stargazers sold for four guilders *per stem*, an astonishing price that reflected just how special they were.

After about eight months of working with lilies, life took another unexpected turn. I came across an advertisement in a horticultural magazine. An American company called Oregon Bulb Farms was looking for a lily grower to help expand their flower program at their facility in Sandy, Oregon.

The idea of going to America felt thrilling, but also unsettling. It was so far away from everything I had ever known. As fate would have it, the president of the company was in Holland for the lily show at Keukenhof. An interview was set up at the office of Homme Mantel, one of the owners of ABM, a respected bulb trading company.

I still remember walking into that office, nervous but determined, facing Homme Mantel and George Heublein, the president of Oregon Bulb Farms. The questions came quickly, and in English. I must admit, my English at the time was terrible. I loved math, science, and biology in school, but language classes were never my strong suit. Somehow, despite my broken sentences and awkward grammar, I muddled through the interview. And to my astonishment, they offered me the job!

The plan was for me to move to Sandy, Oregon, and help build up Oregon Bulb Farms' lily flowering program. It took nearly the entire summer of 1983 to finalize the paperwork and get my visa. Thus, on October 23, 1983, I boarded a plane at Schiphol Airport, suitcase in hand and heart pounding with excitement and anticipation. The first flight took me to London Gatwick, then on to Minneapolis with Northwest Orient Airlines. My final destination was supposed to be Portland, Oregon.

As the plane lifted off, I carried more than just a suitcase. I carried with me generations of flower growing, a restless spirit, and a sense, quiet but certain, that there was a greater purpose waiting for me across the ocean, a brand-new world waiting for me on the other side.

CHAPTER 2

THE AMERICAN DREAM EMBODIED

Man's rise or fall, success or failure, Happiness of unhappiness depends on his attitude…A man's attitude will create the situation he imagines.

AMERICAN NOVELIST JAMES ALLEN

The flight from Amsterdam to London was delayed, and I missed my connection. Thus, my journey took a slightly different route, from London to Minneapolis, then on to Seattle, and finally, one last flight to Portland, Oregon. Late that night I arrived at my destination. Eddy McCrae, Oregon Bulb Farms' lead hybridizer at the time, picked me up from the airport and drove me to the farm. I spent my first night in a small company apartment located at the farm in Sandy, Oregon.

For a few days after my arrival the weather was beautiful with clear skies and crisp mornings. It felt like a warm welcome to a new chapter in my life. That first week gave me hope that perhaps Oregon was exactly the fresh start I had dreamed about.

But then the rain came. And it didn't just come, it stayed. It rained and rained, day after day. Each morning, we drove 35 minutes from the Sandy farm to Oregon Bulb Farms' greenhouse operation in Canby. It felt like we were driving through an aquarium, the rain pounding endlessly against the windshield. At the time, I didn't realize it, but we were experiencing one of the wettest falls on record in Oregon, thanks to a relentless series of atmospheric rivers. It felt as though the sun had simply disappeared.

Once I started working inside the greenhouse, the reality of the situation became clear. I quickly realized why they had been looking for someone who knew a little more about growing lilies than the expertise that was present at the time.

Oregon Bulb Farms had leased an old greenhouse from Crown Zellerbach, a timber company that had once used the space to raise conifer seedlings for reforestation. The greenhouse was covered in fiberglass, and it was probably more than 30 years old.

Years of exposure to sun, wind, dust, and rain had badly weathered the fiberglass. Dirt had settled deep into the pores and cracks, dulling the panels. This wasn't just an aging greenhouse, it was a heavily shaded, almost dark environment.

Inside, rows of benches, each about three feet high, stood where the conifer seedlings had once grown. Oregon Bulb Farms had placed plastic crates filled with soil on top of these benches and planted lily bulbs in them. In theory, it wasn't a bad idea. But theory and reality are often two very different things, especially when you're dealing with plants that depend on light.

By the time I arrived, we were well into October. With heavy clouds overhead and rain falling day after day, the darkness inside the greenhouse was extreme. As a result, most of the lilies had aborted their buds.

There was only one exception, a yellow variety called *Sunray* that somehow tolerated the conditions and managed to bloom. But for the rest, it was a disaster. The buds dried up, shriveled, and the lilies became completely unsellable.

And so, I spent my first weeks in Oregon doing something I hadn't exactly envisioned—pulling dead lilies out of crates and throwing them into dumpsters. It wasn't glamorous. It wasn't easy. But it was real and it also was a lesson.

Sometimes the first step toward building something meaningful isn't success, it's seeing clearly what doesn't work. And sometimes purpose doesn't reveal itself in a grand moment; it starts quietly, humbly, pulling dead lilies from the soil, learning what not to do, and slowly, stubbornly planting the seeds for something better.

George Heublein tasked me with contacting greenhouse builders in Holland to design a new lily-growing operation, a greenhouse of about 100,000 square feet, to be built in the Canby, Oregon, region. One thing had become crystal clear to me: with all the rain in Oregon, it would have to be a glass greenhouse, not fiberglass, to maximize the transmission of light. We would also need grow lights for the winter months. Without them, success would be impossible.

Shortly after settling into my role at Sandy, I found a place to live in Gresham, a suburb of Portland, at a semi-boarding house shared by five young guys and run by an older lady, Mrs. Suminski, who cooked dinner for us every night. The arrangement was simple, and the food was great, a small comfort while adjusting to a new country and a new life.

At Oregon Bulb Farms, the workday ended sharply at 4:00 p.m. each day. I wanted to work longer hours and wanted to stay busy, but company rules forbade anyone from working past that set time. After coming from a background of long farm days back home, I found myself restless, looking for something more.

I checked around with other nurseries in the area, hoping to pick up extra hours or work on Saturdays, but there were no opportunities. For a while, I was frustrated, not sure what to do with the idle time.

Then, one Saturday while driving through Gresham, I noticed something that stirred a memory from home. There were willow trees everywhere, big, healthy trees in many yards.

It brought me back to cold winter nights in Holland, when our family would pick pussy willow branches from the hedgerows surrounding our farm. We would bring them into the house, warm them up by the fireplace, and spend hours peeling the outer skins from the buds on the stems to create perfectly manicured bunches. They were used for Christmas arrangements and mixed with daffodils in January, a simple but beautiful tradition that tied family and farm life together.

Maybe, I thought, there was a way to bring a piece of that tradition to Oregon. So, on Saturdays, I started stopping at people's houses, ringing doorbells, and offering to trim and prune their willow trees. Most homeowners were happy to have someone take care of it, and I was happy for the chance to work. I would haul the branches back to Mrs. Suminski's basement, where I stored my growing inventory.

Each evening, I would take a fresh bundle upstairs, lay them in front of the fireplace, and peel the skins off by hand, just like we did back in Holland. It was slow work, but satisfying. It gave me something familiar to hold onto while everything else around me was so new. Mrs. Suminski would watch with a mix of curiosity and admiration. At one point she smiled and said, "Someday, you'll be driving a Cadillac."

Once I had enough bunches prepared, I took them to the flower market in Portland, arriving early enough in the morning so that I could get back in time to start the day at Oregon Bulb Farms. The first few times, it worked well enough, but there was one problem: many wholesalers didn't pay immediately. Some wanted to pay on 30-day terms, and that didn't sit too well with me.

I had put in the work, the care, the patience, and I wanted to be paid right away. And once again, I found myself faced with a choice: accept the way things were or find a different way. That small internal push, that unwillingness to stand still, was part of a deeper quest already beginning to take root inside. That quest was a pursuit of purpose, of independence, of building a future with my own two hands.

In my feisty demeanor, I decided it was time to change my approach. I grabbed a Portland phonebook, flipped to the yellow pages, and started scrolling through the list of florists, putting dots on a map to mark where each one was located across the city. The next Saturday, I loaded up the pickup truck with bunches of carefully prepared pussy willows and set out.

One by one, I visited the florists on my map, walking in with my bundles in hand. It was an interesting experience, most of the florists were impressed with the quality, and best of all, they paid me right away, cash in hand. There was something incredibly satisfying about it, not just making the sale, but realizing that with a little grit and creativity, I could carve out my own path, even in a place where everything was still new to me.

It wasn't just about selling flowers, it was about finding a way forward, about building something real, one bunch at a time. That little side hustle gave me a renewed sense of purpose. Even while working within the structure and rules of Oregon Bulb Farms, I realized that my spirit was wired for building, for creating something new. It was a small reminder that no matter where I was planted, I could find a way to grow.

Not long after, a quiet buzz began to build around the office, rumors of something much bigger on the horizon.

I began to overhear conversations about a potential acquisition of a company called Sun Valley Bulb Farms, located in Arcata, California. There was a noticeable spirit of excitement around the office. Oregon Bulb Farms was still relatively small when I joined. The president's office (George Heublein), the CFO's office, and the sales manager's office were all within about 30 feet of each other, so it was easy to pick up on the discussions swirling around.

I started wondering: where exactly was Arcata? I pulled out my Rand McNally atlas, the one I had brought with me from Holland, filled with maps of all the U.S. states, and began searching. I found Arcata tucked away along the Northern California coast, just north of Humboldt Bay. Curious, I dug deeper and began studying the climate data.

The Willamette Valley, where Oregon Bulb Farms was located, experienced very warm summers, with daytime temperatures often well into the 80s and 90s, and cold, dark winters, frequently dropping to freezing temperatures.

It was good growing country for many crops, but not ideal for lilies, which need moderate conditions and plenty of light.

When I searched for Arcata's climate data, I found reports for nearby Eureka, California, only seven miles south of Arcata, and which shared the same coastal climate. What I found surprised me. The summers in Arcata were mild, with average temperatures in August around 63°F, obviously much cooler than the Willamette Valley. While Arcata also received a fair amount of winter rainfall, the total precipitation wasn't all that different from Canby. But there was one critical difference.

Arcata, sitting farther south at 41 degrees latitude (comparable to Naples, Italy), enjoyed significantly better light levels. And because it was right on the coast, even when winter storms came through, there were more breaks between the storms, more moments when the sun could break through. In contrast, the northern Willamette Valley often endured one storm after another, creating a seemingly endless blanket of clouds.

The more I compared the data, the clearer it became: Arcata had a far superior climate for growing lilies. I gathered all my findings and put together a climate comparison report. Then, one day, I walked into George Heublein's office, report in hand.

"Mr. Heublein," I said, "I understand there's talk about a potential purchase of Sun Valley Bulb Farms. If that were to happen, here's a report I would like you to consider. When you compare the climate conditions of Arcata to the Northern Willamette Valley, Arcata is by far the better location for growing lilies."

It felt like a small moment, but a significant one. I was still new, still trying to find my place. But offering that report was a way of stepping forward, of adding value, of planting the seeds of a bigger future not just for myself, but for what might come next. And in that simple act, a deeper sense of purpose began to quietly take hold.

George Heublein looked over the report carefully, then told me on the spot, "If we buy Sun Valley, and at this point it still isn't certain, if we buy it, that's where we'll build the greenhouse." That moment felt like a turning point. A small idea I had chased down with a map and a little curiosity now had the potential to shape the future of the company and my own path.

Next thing I knew, on January 10, 1984, I found myself heading south on an expedition trip to Sun Valley. I traveled with Ed Hobbs, a manager at Oregon Bulb Farms, and Matt van der Linden, the company's incumbent lily grower. Our job was to conduct due diligence and report our findings back to George Heublein.

When we arrived at Sun Valley, Ted Kirsch, one of the owners who was in the process of selling his business, invited us to dinner at his home. But to my surprise, the three of us didn't all have dinner together. The first night, Ted and his wife Eloise invited only me over for dinner. The second night, Matt and Ed went together.

At the time, I thought it was a little odd. Why have separate dinners? Why not all of us at once? Weeks later, it became clear: these weren't just friendly meals, they were job interviews in disguise. I remember those conversations vividly. We talked at length about the specifics of growing lilies and tulips, about the different types of greenhouses we should consider for the future. The discussions went deep into finances, like cost price calculations, cost accounting, depreciation schedules, and much more.

Apparently, I made an impression. Because not long after, I learned I had been selected, the one chosen to be sent from Oregon to California to set up the greenhouse operation for lilies at the newly acquired Sun Valley farm.

On the way back to Oregon, we made a stop in Myrtle Point, a remote valley in Southern Oregon where Sun Valley had originally started back in 1948. Even in 1983 that farm was still active, growing daffodils in the winter and volunteer iris in the spring on about 60 acres.

It was humble, out of the way, and deeply rooted in tradition. Standing there, seeing where it had all begun, left an impression on me. It was a reminder that big dreams often take root in small, unlikely places. From Myrtle Point, we drove back to Gresham, finally arriving late that night.

The next day turned out to be one of my last Saturdays in Oregon. I was bound for Arcata, California, ready to step into a new future. The irony wasn't lost on me: by the time I left I was making more money selling pussy willows each week than I earned on my paycheck at Oregon Bulb Farms.

But somehow, I could feel something deeper unfolding. It had never been just about the paycheck. It was about the pursuit of opportunity. It was about building something real. And more than anything, it was about stepping toward a life of purpose, one step, one decision, one lily at a time.

CHAPTER 3

ARCATA BOUND

*I've always believed that success for anyone is
all about drive, dedication, and desire.*

STEPHEN CURRY

On January 23, 1984, I was off to Arcata. When I arrived at Sun Valley, the farm was in the midst of its daffodil harvest. In those days, daffodils were the largest crop at Sun Valley. The Myrtle Point farm produced about 3 million stems each season; the Arcata farm produced close to 11 million stems.

After the bulbs were dug up during the summer, they were cooled at 48 degrees and then replanted in October. The first variety to bloom was *Fortune*, flowering as early as the end of November and hitting full production by December. By early January, the precooled *Dutch Masters* would come in, followed by the *volunteer* Dutch Masters around the third week of January. *Volunteers* was the term we used for bulbs that had stayed in the ground for an additional year.

By the time I arrived, the crews were deep into the volunteer Dutch Master harvest. The climate for growing daffodils in Arcata was ideal: mild, wet winters and cool summers, very much like the southern part of England, where daffodil growing had been perfected over centuries.

I vividly remember some of the ups and downs of daffodil production in those days. When the weather stayed dry, and we had frost in the mornings, the daffodils would just sit there, stubbornly refusing to grow. We would try our best to fill orders, but it was difficult to hit the numbers, and the stems we picked were getting shorter and shorter due to the lack of water. We even tried irrigating the fields, but it didn't help much. Nature has its own timing, and sometimes, no amount of work or worry could change it.

But when a *Pineapple Express* rolled in, everything would change overnight. *Pineapple Express* storms are Pacific storms that originate near Hawaii, bringing warm, moisture-rich air to the coast. Before they arrived, nighttime temperatures would rise sharply, and it would stay warm day and night, often into the upper 60s and low 70s. When a Pineapple Express hit, the daffodils would break loose, bursting into a frenzy of daffodil flowers almost too fast to control. One day the fields would be quiet and still; the next, they would explode into a sea of buds ready to pick.

The picking crew in those days consisted of about 150 workers. Their pay was based on piecework, seven cents per bunch. During the dry spells the crew sat around wondering what to do, occasionally picking a few very short daffodils just to stay busy. But when the Pineapple Express storms arrived, we could be picking 400,000 daffodils a day and still struggle to keep up. It was nerve-racking to say the least, but it was exhilarating too, a reminder that when the opportunity arrives, you have to be ready to move fast. After the daffodil season wound down, things would grow quiet for a few weeks. The last variety we picked was *Standard Value*, which wrapped up by the end of February.

By mid-March, the first iris varieties would begin to bloom; *Wedgwood* and *White Wedgwood* came first, followed by *Ideal*. The big push came in April, with lots of *Blue Ribbon* (known in Holland as *Professor Blauw*), which was the main variety in those days. The iris season finished by the first week of May with late varieties like *Hildegarde*, *Imperator*, and *Golden Harvest*.

Sun Valley was already well-known by then for its spring iris program. The iris were grown as *volunteers*, meaning the bulbs stayed in the ground and returned year after year, sometimes for up to ten years. The climate that made Arcata perfect for lilies and daffodils also proved ideal for iris. Because the summers never got too hot, and because California summers were dry, we could leave the bulbs in the ground without worry. In many other places, bulbs would rot from summer moisture or freeze out in harsh winters.

Once the iris leaves naturally died back by August, we would pass a large field burner slowly over the fields, burning off the dead foliage and any weeds that had emerged. It was a simple but effective system, relying on nature's own rhythms to reset the field for the next season. By October, the iris would break dormancy and start pushing their leaves out of the ground again. They would grow steadily all winter long, preparing to bloom anywhere from March through early May, depending on the variety.

Those iris were shipped all over the country. I remember the early days when Sun Valley put together its own dedicated trucks for flower shipments. It was a bold move at the time. In the 1980s, most flowers grown in California were shipped by air freight. Shipping from California by truck was still a relatively new phenomenon back then but it was a sign of innovation and a commitment to finding better ways to serve the market. Looking back, I realize now that Sun Valley's success wasn't just about good crops or good timing, it was also about being willing to think differently.

As the spring iris season wound down and the fields began to quiet again, a new sense of energy started building at Sun Valley. The farm had deep roots in daffodils and iris, but now the future was calling us toward the construction of the brand-new glass greenhouse, and with it, the launch of a full-scale lily program. For me personally, it was another step deeper into the pursuit of purpose that had first carried me across the Atlantic. What lay ahead wouldn't be easy, but it would be a chance to help build something new from the ground up. That was exactly the kind of opportunity I had been hoping for.

The soil in Arcata was heavy clay, perfect for growing daffodils and iris, but far from ideal for lilies in a greenhouse setting. During the summer of 1984, we began prepping one of the fields for the new project. We sourced sand from a local farmer whose property bordered sand dunes, and where strong northwest winds in the spring blew sand into his fields. We hauled in a layer of sand about two feet thick, spreading it across the heavy clay. Once the sand was in place, we installed a drainage system to make sure excess water could properly flow away.

By July 1984, we began construction on our first major greenhouse, a 110,000-square-foot glasshouse. And by December of that same year, we picked the first lilies from it. It wasn't an easy start. There were plenty of stumbles along the way, but we were off to the races, nonetheless. In that first year, we grew only Asiatic lilies in the new glasshouse.

Behind this greenhouse, we rebuilt a gutter-connected hoophouse that had previously been dismantled and sent down from Oregon Bulb Farms. We planted Rubrum lilies in that hoophouse. Unfortunately, the boiler needed to heat the greenhouse was terribly delayed. While Asiatic lilies can handle cooler winter conditions reasonably well, Rubrums cannot, and they struggled badly without the required heat. It was another hard-earned lesson in the long process of building something new.

Before we built the large greenhouse the only existing greenhouse on the Arcata farm was a wide-span, single-bay greenhouse of less than 10,000 square feet; It was nicknamed *Big Bertha*. Sun Valley had been using it to grow Alstroemeria, specifically the *Rosario* variety. Given my background with tulips, it made sense to pivot. We decided *Big Bertha* would become the launching pad for Sun Valley's tulip program. The Alstroemeria came out, and tulips went in.

The first year, we imported two containers of tulip bulbs. One container of bulbs was for early forcing, that is, tulips grown in crates for flowering from January through mid-March, inside the wide-span *Big Bertha* greenhouse. The bulbs in the other container were meant to be planted directly into the ground inside one of the cold greenhouses we had reassembled from Oregon.

The simple start of the Sun Valley tulip program in December 1984

The crate-grown tulips flourished. The quality was excellent right from the start: large bulbs, rich soil, and strong, heavy tulips. But the ones planted directly into the ground didn't fare so well. We had assumed the mild winters in Arcata would provide enough natural chilling, much like back home in Holland. We were wrong. The winters in Arcata, although wet, simply didn't get cold enough to satisfy the chilling requirements, and the tulips grew much shorter than they should have. It was a tough but valuable lesson, one that taught us the limits of assuming we could copy a system from one climate to another without adjustments. It was the first, and the last, time we attempted to grow uncooled tulips in an unheated greenhouse.

• • •

That fall, while shopping at a local grocery store, I spotted a sign for a truck giveaway promotion sponsored by a local Toyota dealer and radio station KATA. All I had to do was put my name into a big bin at the front of the store. If the radio station called my name on the air, I had two minutes to phone in and secure a chance to win the truck. It sounded like a fun idea, so I dropped my name in. Lo and behold, one day while listening to the radio I heard my name called "on the air." I made the phone call within the two-minute window, and before I knew it, I was among 100 contestants, each holding a key and filled with anticipation, standing inside the Toyota dealership.

Each person got a chance to try their key in the truck's ignition, but only one would fit. As I stood there waiting for my turn, I noticed a very attractive girl who worked for the radio station. She caught my eye, and it seemed I had caught hers as well. She kept glancing at me through the crowd, and I couldn't help but glance back. Eventually, it was my turn to try the key. It didn't fit. I didn't win the truck.

But afterward, I struck up a conversation with this girl. Her name was Kathryn. We hit it off right away, and that day turned out to be far more important than any truck giveaway. Today, I am proud to say Kathryn and I have been married for 39 years. I may not have won the pickup truck that day, but I won something far more valuable: A partner who has stood by me through every season of life, through every challenge, and through every dream we built together.

Looking back now, it's clear that those early days in Arcata were about far more than just building a greenhouse or starting flower programs. They were about building something deeper, a future shaped by faith, hard work, and a steady pursuit of purpose. And somehow, along the way, life had given me not just a new beginning, but a partner to share the journey with.

CHAPTER 4

RAPID GROWTH, 1985 TO 1988

If you're trying to achieve, there will be roadblocks. I've had
them; everybody has them. But obstacles don't have to stop
you. If you run into a wall, don't turn around and give up.
Figure out how to climb it, go through it, or work around it.

MICHAEL JORDAN

M elridge Inc., the newly formed parent company of Oregon Bulb
Farms, and by now the owner of Sun Valley, was publicly traded
on the NASDAQ stock exchange. In 1985 and 1986, Melridge
made a number of acquisitions, expanding aggressively. Meanwhile, under
the Melridge umbrella, Sun Valley was growing rapidly as well.

In 1985, we selected another field and prepared it for building another new
greenhouse, again hauling in enough sand to cover the field with two feet of
sand over the heavy clay soil. We then built another glass greenhouse, this one
at 165,000 square feet, imported from a Dutch company called *Prins Dok-*
kum. That same year, we also built a 27,000-square-foot warehouse, complete
with a mezzanine area. After visiting several major flower shipping companies

35

in the San Francisco Bay Area in 1985, we adopted their concept of storing cardboard and boxes on a mezzanine above the packing area. It turned out to be an extremely efficient way to use space and improve the flow of work in the packing operation.

The new warehouse was situated right in the middle of the farm, allowing product from the greenhouses and fields to flow into a single central location for processing, packing, and shipping. To protect the quality of our flowers, we did some research into precooling systems, traveling to Indio, California, to study techniques that preserved flower integrity without dehydrating them before shipment. It was a small but important investment in the future and in protecting the reputation we were working so hard to build.

In 1986, we added another 165,000 square feet of greenhouse space, again following the same process, laying down sand for drainage and making the ground suitable for growing lilies. This time, the sand came from an unusual source. In 1979, the Army Corps of Engineers had completed a bay-deepening project, pumping an estimated 500,000 yards of dredged sand into a natural depression among the coastal dunes on the Samoa Peninsula, a 20-minute

The 1984 greenhouse on the right, 1985 and 1986 greenhouse on the left, with the new warehouse in the center.

drive from the farm. The site, nicknamed the "Superbowl," had sat untouched for years. We arranged to haul sand from the Superbowl to our fields. It was quite a spectacle, eight dump trucks working full-time, hauling load after load to the farm.

By the end of 1986, we had built 440,000 square feet of glass greenhouses in just three years. It was an incredible pace of growth, driven by opportunity, and supported by a deep belief that we were building something bigger than ourselves. Most of the greenhouse space was used for growing Asiatic lilies, such as Oregon Bulb Farms' varieties *Edith, Impala, Pollyanna, Sunflight, Foxtrot, Oreglow, Firebrand, Alpenglow, Zephyr, Colleen*, and *Sterling Star*.

We also grew Oriental lilies such as *Stargazer, San Souci, Imperial Crimson*, and *White Dream*, alongside an expanding tulip program.

The tulip program grew from about one million stems in the first winter to roughly three million stems by the third year. Early on, part of the tulip program relied on *5-degree* tulips, bulbs that had received all their cooling (at 41F) before planting. This eliminated the need for cooler space, which we had very little of during the early years. However, growing precooled tulips directly in the greenhouses came with challenges. In years when we had a cold November or December, the bulbs rooted properly, and the crops performed well. But in years with warm winters, especially when a Pineapple Express hit during winter, we faced havoc, like softrot, root rot, and premature blooming that led to shorter tulips. Eventually the construction of additional cooler space solved this dilemma.

For several seasons we also tried growing tulips outdoors in the fields, planting them in the fall to bloom in March. At first, it seemed promising. But we quickly learned that growing field tulips carried its own risks. The region often experiences hail during spring storms, and the broad leaves of tulips are particularly vulnerable to hail damage. To counter this, we began planting the field tulips inside shade houses, which offered some protection from the weather.

Still, the bigger problem was the unpredictability of the crop's timing.

During March, we would scale back greenhouse tulip production, expecting the field crop to come in. But with a cold spring, the field tulips would be late, leaving us with short supply. If the spring were warm, the field tulips would come too early, overlapping with the last flushes of greenhouse production.

The field tulip program was a logistical juggling act, and an unreliable one at that. After about five years we decided to stop it. Without the field program, we could plan and manage greenhouse production far more effectively, delivering a much more dependable crop to our customers.

The trials and tribulations of the early tulip program, whether it was planting uncooled bulbs in an unheated greenhouse, managing the warm winter setbacks on the 5-degree program, or enduring five years of experimentation with field-grown tulips, all served as essential building blocks. Each challenge taught us something. And together, these challenges laid the foundation for the strong and resilient tulip program that would emerge in the years to come.

By the end of 1986, Sun Valley had taken huge strides forward, from a small coastal farm to a rapidly growing flower company with new greenhouses, better systems, and big ambitions. Little did we know at the time that storm clouds were already gathering above our parent company.

CHAPTER 5

MELRIDGE

When pride comes, then comes disgrace,
but with humility comes wisdom.

PROVERBS11:2

M elridge, the parent company, continued on a very fast growth trajectory. Not only was it expanding at the Sun Valley location, it had also built a brand-new warehouse in Canby, Oregon, for the Oregon Bulb Farms division, where all the lily bulbs were grown.

It also purchased a flower exporter in Holland called *van den Adel*, and it owned *Sun Pacific Flower Shippers*, a brokerage business that marketed and sold mostly daffodils and tulips grown by farms throughout the Pacific Northwest. Melridge acquired *ABM*, the bulb brokerage business in Holland, where I originally had been interviewed for a job.

By 1987, Melridge had expanded even further. It owned a flower farm in Burundi, Africa, and had acquired a carnation farm in Spain, *Primores S.A.* In the United States, it bought six flower wholesalers and rebranded them all as *SunFlor Wholesale*, with locations in San Francisco, Los Angeles, Dallas, Seattle, Phoenix, and Portland, Oregon. It also acquired a 50% stake in

Conroy's, a large retail florist chain based in Los Angeles, and launched *Sun Atlantic Flower Shippers*, which operated from Valley Stream, New York.

It is no understatement to say that George Heublein, the flamboyant and charismatic CEO, was flying high during these years. He was featured on

the cover of several magazines, including *Vakblad voor de Bloemisterij*, the leading Dutch horticultural weekly. In one particularly memorable interview, he proclaimed that someday Melridge would be bigger than the VBA, the largest flower auction in the world at the time. Unsurprisingly, such grandiose statements caused a stir, and plenty of ridicule throughout the flower industry.

As a young twenty-something-year-old kid from Holland, all of this made a profound and lasting impression on me. It became a life lesson

George Heublein

that reinforced a premise my parents had taught me years earlier: No matter what happens, even when apparent success comes your way, always remain humble and gracious. Do not boast. *"Let another praise you, and not your own mouth; a stranger, and not your own lips."* (Proverbs 27:2) (This principle is later reflected on in the "Guiding Principles" section of this book.)

Ultimately, the hubris, the self-aggrandizement, and the relentless drive to build a large publicly traded empire caught up with George Heublein and his executive team. The trouble began when Gary Wood, the CFO at the time, suffered a heart attack and was replaced by an outsider. The new CFO quickly uncovered serious fraudulent behavior inside Melridge' s management. The house of cards came tumbling down and by December 1988, Melridge had to file for bankruptcy.

When we built our first greenhouse, at 110,000 square feet, it cost roughly $700,000 to construct. The second, in 1985, was 165,000 square feet and came in at about $1.1 million, which made sense given the typical cost of greenhouse construction in those days. But I never understood how the same size greenhouse built in 1986 ended up costing more than $2,000,000. After Melridge filed for bankruptcy in December 1988, an astonishing behind-the scenes story finally came to light about what had actually taken place. To this day, it's hard to comprehend how Price Waterhouse, the auditing firm at the time, failed to catch what was going on

Oregon Bulb Farms was active in hybridizing lilies, with many new varieties emerging from its pipeline. These patented varieties were typically grown by Oregon Bulb Farms itself or sold to other bulb growers, including growers in the Netherlands. In conjunction with this hybridizing program, and in addition to the sale of shares in this publicly traded company, Heublein and his team had devised another method for generating additional funding to support their ambitious growth strategy.

Heublein had come up with a concept of selling varieties as a collection within a partnership structure, which became known as "The Partnership Varieties." Two such partnerships were established. The idea was that investors would purchase partnership shares, and the varieties would be grown by bulb growers in the Netherlands, who paid royalties for the right to grow them. Those royalties would generate revenue for the partnership. This royalty income was then paid out to investors in the form of dividend payments.

On the surface, it seemed like an interesting concept. There was only one problem—many of these "partnership" varieties didn't perform very well. As a result, interest from bulb growers in Holland to expand acreage was minimal. In order to maintain a positive narrative for the investors in these partnerships, management was compelled to portray the varieties as highly lucrative. They were determined to preserve the illusion of Melridge as a profitable and thriving company, no matter the underlying reality.

Now, back to my confusion over why the 1986 greenhouse ended up costing more than $2 million. Court documents eventually revealed the truth. The actual cost of the greenhouse was still $1.1 million, but the Dutch manufacturer was instructed to issue an invoice for double that amount. Melridge paid the full $2.2 million, and the manufacturer was directed to wire the $1.1 million difference to a Swiss bank account.

Surprisingly, the greenhouse manufacturer went along with the scheme and transferred the funds to the Swiss bank account as instructed. From there, the money was funneled back to the United States, disguised as "royalty payments for the partnership varieties." It was a financial shell game designed to mask the growing problems inside the company.

This arrangement wasn't limited to just the Arcata greenhouse. Melridge had also purchased a substantial amount of machinery in Holland for its Oregon Bulb Farms division, and those transactions were subjected to the same fraudulent manipulation.

After Gary Wood's abrupt, medically-related departure, the new CFO took time to familiarize himself with the position. But soon after, things began to unravel rapidly. George Heublein was indicted for fraud and fled the country, but was eventually apprehended and arrested in Florida. In 1997, he was sentenced to five years in federal prison. He has since passed away.

Melridge was structured with numerous direct subsidiaries, including Oregon Bulb Farms, Joe Berger and Co., the SunFlor wholesale houses, and several others, all of which were directly tied to the federal bankruptcy filing. However, the way the Sun Valley Bulb Farms acquisition had been structured meant that it retained its own separate legal status and, as a result, was not included in the 1988 bankruptcy proceedings.

Meanwhile, with its two Dutch subsidiaries, ABM and van den Adel, Melridge had established a significant presence in the Netherlands under the banner of "Melridge Holland." A man named Harry van Achteren served as the CFO of that division.

After Melridge filed for bankruptcy, van Achteren and Ton Augustinus (one of the former owners of ABM) put together a reorganization plan and launched a new entity called "Global Floral." This new company was composed of Oregon Bulb Farms, Sun Pacific, and Sun Valley in the U.S., along with ABM in Holland.

However, *Global Floral* assumed 100% of the debt left behind by Melridge, while holding very little equity of its own. Over the next 22 months, it would become painfully clear that this debt structure was simply not sustainable, and it would test every lesson I had learned up to that point about resilience, humility, and perseverance.

CHAPTER 6

GLOBAL FLORAL

Nothing in the world is worth having or worth doing
unless it means effort, pain, difficulty...I don't envy
people who lead an easy life. I have envied a great many
people who led difficult lives and led them well.

THEODORE ROOSEVELT

G lobal Floral officially commenced as a company on February 15, 1989. But from day one, it was clear this new venture was doomed to fail. I will never forget when Harry van Achteren came to Arcata with his assistant, Ramona. He invited my controller and me out to dinner. During the meal, he started explaining that our accounts payable were currently about 20 days outstanding. Harry told us he was planning to stretch that out to 90 days. By doing so, he explained, we would "create" $1.6 million in liquidity. My controller and I looked at each other, rolled our eyes, and right there, right then, we knew we were in for trouble.

Harry had formulated an extremely aggressive growth strategy. At the time (1989), Sun Valley was producing about 450,000 Asiatic lilies a month. As a means to increase cash flow, the directive from Harry was to push production to one million stems a month. However, there wasn't really any accompanying sales or marketing plan to absorb the additional flowers.

For the winter months, Global leased a greenhouse location in Encinitas, California. It also leased ground from an Amaryllis grower in Santa Maria. And during the summer, the plan was to harvest additional lilies from the bulb fields at Oregon Bulb Farms. The result was predictable: A massive glut of lilies flooded the market, saturating it and driving prices down. Instead of creating more cash flow, the opposite happened, as losses piled up and market credibility reached an all-time low.

The Global Floral saga dragged on for 22 months. Finally, on December 11, 1990, Harry van Achteren filed for Chapter 11 bankruptcy protection in federal court in Eugene, Oregon. This time, unlike the Melridge collapse, Sun Valley was directly involved.

Harry asked me to attend the court proceedings and help make the case for the bank to provide cash collateral to keep operations afloat. The court hearing started at 4:00 p.m. and lasted until 11:00 p.m. that night. The judge pressed late into the evening because the next day the courthouse would be closed as protesters were expected to block access in response to the impending 1990–1991 Gulf War.

The good news was that the judge granted cash collateral for several weeks. The bad news: every single expenditure, even basic operational costs such as payroll, had to be pre-approved by the attorneys representing the bank. Only the most essential payments would be allowed. Each week we had to submit a funding request for payroll. Each week, the uncertainty and tension mounted.

One week, it wasn't until Friday morning at 10:00 a.m. that the money was finally released into the payroll account, just hours before checks were due to go out. The following week, I decided to press the issue early. We calculated the anticipated needs, communicated everything clearly to our bankruptcy attorneys, and followed up repeatedly. But as the days dragged on, my anxiety grew. Things ultimately came to a boiling point on the last day of that week.

Friday, January 25, 1991, is a day I will never forget as long as I live. Mid-morning I had a call with our attorneys and the attorneys of the bank. They kept on talking and trying to find reasons not to pay the wages of our team members for the previous week. They were hinting that payroll might be withheld for the week. At that point I lost my cool and rebuked them with much emotion: you guys are sitting there in a nice corner office on the twentieth floor in Portland in your leather chairs and your expensive suits, and you think you can just deny these people their paychecks? These people work hard to make a living; they are counting on their paycheck at four o'clock this afternoon. If you don't allow the money to get wired so we can pay our people, there may be a riot out here.

And as you may sit there comfortably in your office and you presume that your assets are secure, guess what, at the end of the day, I can't guarantee what will happen to your assets if these people don't get paid. What you own here is a large 440,000 square feet of greenhouse built out of glass, glass that can easily break. You know what could happen when people get angry, there may not be much glass left in those greenhouses by the end of the day. DO YOU UNDERSTAND THAT???

There was a long silence on the phone that seemed to last for minutes. Finally, one of the bank's attorneys calmly said: "We got your point." They promised they would fund the payroll account that afternoon. The clock kept ticking and by 4:00 p.m. the workday had ended for our team; it was time to give out the paychecks for the week. However, the money still had not arrived in the account, so we could not give out the checks. Finally, by 5:30 p.m. the funds finally arrived into our payroll account, and we handed out the paychecks. However, by then it was too late for many to cash their checks as the banks closed at 6:00 p.m. In those days the banks were also open on Saturday mornings, so we gave all the team members time to cash their checks the next morning,

On Saturday at 11:00 am I called a companywide meeting. I explained to the team the precarious situation we were in and that we had fought to get the checks released for everyone. That following Monday I was on my way to Portland for a series of meetings and a hearing in bankruptcy court. The mission was to secure funding for a more extensive time period.

By now the case had been moved from Eugene to the Portland federal bankruptcy court. The hearing in Portland turned out as I had hoped. We made the case that even though "Global Floral" was the debtor and the company that had filed for bankruptcy, Sun Valley was a profitable entity and deserved to continue and conduct business as usual.

With Valentines Day only three weeks away, the judge granted us the cash collateral with less restrictions, which gave us the ability to continue to pay vendors for the services we needed to keep the enterprise going. By the time I drove home from Portland on Friday night that week, I had a huge sense of relief, and a feeling of accomplishment filled my whole being. Above all, I praised God in Heaven for placing us in the palm of his hands, for carrying us through the storm, and saving our company.

CHAPTER 7

A NEW PATH FORWARD

I can't change the direction of the wind, but I can
adjust my sails to always reach my destination.

JIMMY DEAN

The judge appointed a Chapter 11 trustee to oversee Sun Valley's case. The trustee's name was Michael Batlan. Meanwhile, for Oregon Bulb Farms, which had been a financial drain for years, the judge appointed a separate Chapter 7 trustee, tasked with liquidating that business.

Michael and I hit it off right away. He came to Arcata to see firsthand what we were doing, the crops we grew, the team atmosphere we had built, the culture that had developed at Sun Valley. We invited him to one of our monthly farm meetings. He gave a speech to the team and because of his visit quickly understood the spirit that kept the company alive. Together, we began plotting a path for the continuation of Sun Valley.

When Harry van Achteren had first filed for bankruptcy, he had hired an expert appraiser from Holland, a man with an impeccable reputation for appraising farms for Dutch lenders. His name was Jacob Rooijakkers. Jacob was in his late 50s, a well-respected man full of wisdom and experience. He and his family, his brother, three sons, and three nephews owned and operated a large bulb farm in Breezand, Holland, where they grew lilies, tulips, and iris.

Coincidentally, Jacob was already familiar with Sun Valley. Back in 1976, he and another Dutchman, Aad de Bruin, had spotted the *Stargazer* lily growing in the fields at Arcata. Jacob was one of the very first bulb growers to grow *Stargazer* lilies in Holland. Jacob also coordinated the *Telstar Group*, a cooperative of 18 iris bulb growers licensed to produce the popular *Telstar* variety. He had a fine eye for spotting promising new varieties of tulips, irises, and lilies.

Jacob arrived in the United States in January 1991 to appraise the assets of Oregon Bulb Farms and Sun Valley. He and I hit it off immediately. We spent many hours talking about growing iris, lilies, and tulips; about the business; about Sun Valley's intrinsic value; and about the possible paths forward.

At one point, Jacob asked me what I thought Sun Valley was worth. I grabbed a yellow legal pad and started jotting down all the assets, estimating their values one by one. By now, Michael Batlan had convinced the judge that Sun Valley should continue operating until a buyer could be found. Since the company was profitable, and did not require outside funding, it was a logical decision.

Over the next several months an idea was born: We would collectively purchase the Sun Valley assets out of the bankruptcy estate. By the fall of 1991, Jacob suggested bringing in another well-respected bulb grower and hybridizer from Breezand to join the venture. His name was Jan van der Wereld. In the first week of November 1991, Jan and Jacob came to Arcata. We spent a few days visiting, talking, walking the farm, and then drove north to Portland for a critical meeting. We sat down with Mike Batlan and our new attorney, John Dirkheimer, to negotiate the details of a potential purchase.

Some of the discussions were intense. Jan didn't speak much English, and at one point, he had enough of all the talking. He quietly got up and went outside to smoke a cigarette. Everyone around the table panicked, fearing that Jan's abrupt departure meant the deal had fallen apart. In a way, his silence worked in our favor. The urgency in the room changed.

After four long days of negotiations, on Friday night, November 15, 1991, we drove back to Arcata with a consummated deal. On Monday, November 18, 1991, the purchase became official. Sun Valley had been saved.

CHAPTER 8

SUN VALLEY
FLORAL FARMS

*The quality of our life is in direct proportion
to our commitment to excellence.*

VINCE LOMBARDI

The deal to purchase Sun Valley was financed with a three-year, $2 million loan from RABO Bank in Holland. (In 1994, we paid off this loan in full, from the cash flow of the business.) In addition, both Rooijakkers and Jan van der Wereld each provided loan funding to the tune of $500,000. Jan van der Wereld was instrumental in ensuring equal ownership in the new venture for all three partners.

One of our first decisions was to change the name of the company. For four decades it had been known as Sun Valley Bulb Farms, a fitting name in the early years when the farm focused on bulb production alongside flower production. But by the 1990s, Sun Valley was no longer in the business of growing or selling bulbs. It was time for a new identity. We renamed the company Sun Valley Floral Farms.

It wasn't just a name change, it marked a fresh beginning, a new chapter that reflected who we had become and where we were headed.

For years, we had been closely associated with Oregon Bulb Farms. The Asiatic lilies we grew were from bulbs produced by OBF, which had a significant dry sale business, that is, bulbs sold for the garden trade. The garden trade market was always in search of the largest bulb sizes, and to meet the Labor Day weekend retail push, those bulbs had to be dug early, typically by mid-August. The smaller-sized bulbs, unsuitable for the garden trade, were conveniently sent to Sun Valley.

In flower production, however, the goal is year-round availability, which requires storing bulbs for up to a year at 28°F. Bulbs dug early in August don't lend themselves well to long-term storage. As one might expect, the quality of these bulbs later in the season often suffered, and with that, so did the yield and flower quality.

This dynamic changed dramatically in November 1991. We were no longer the "convenient" outlet for Oregon Bulb Farms bulbs that couldn't be sold elsewhere. From that day forward we could focus on sourcing and growing the best varieties available, from bulbs dug at the proper time, intended for long-term storage, and capable of producing top-quality flowers year-round

Another key aspect of the new venture was that both Rooijakkers and van der Wereld were hybridizers and selectors of new tulip, lily, and iris varieties. With this new collaboration, Sun Valley became the launch pad for introducing their varieties into the U.S. marketplace. One example is a series of lily varieties that Rooijakkers had previously acquired from hybridizer Bischoff Tulleken. These included *Dame Blanche*, *White Stargazer*, *Kyoto*, *Kissproof*, and *Noblesse*.

During the 1992 Summer Olympics in Barcelona the media was buzzing about the U.S. Olympic basketball team, famously dubbed the "Dream Team." We saw an opportunity and launched a marketing campaign positioning these new Oriental lily varieties as Sun Valley's own "Dream Team." For many years, these standout varieties formed the backbone of Sun Valley's Oriental lily program.

Jan van der Wereld was a pioneer in the development of LA hybrids. Some of his early introductions included *Royal Fantasy*, *Royal Dream*, *Royal Highness*, *Royal Perfume*, *Royal Justice*, *Royal Delight*, and *Royal Cinnabar*. In 1995, during our annual Sun Valley Open House held in July, all five members of the Humboldt County Board of Supervisors attended the event. Stan Dixon, the board chair at the time, officially baptized Jan's new pink LA hybrid as "*Royal Humboldt*" in honor of Humboldt County. The naming ceremony was witnessed by a crowd of several thousand visitors who had come out for that year's Open House.

In 1995, we also planted a few bulbs of *Royal Sunset*, a striking bicolor LA hybrid. This variety turned out to be such a standout that it remained a key part of our program for more than 25 years. Sun Valley's role in introducing these new varieties to the American market did not go unnoticed. In fact, it helped to solidify our position as a leader in the lily market. During the 1990s, we began branding all our LA hybrids under the "Royals" name, and soon after, Sun Valley received a registered trademark for "Royal Lilies" from the U.S. Trademark Office.

As I mentioned earlier, Jacob Rooijakkers was one of the growers and the coordinator of the Telstar iris group. This connection gave us a direct pipeline to the Telstar iris supply. The variety *Telstar* had been hybridized and selected by G.D. Hommes in 1971, and it quickly stood out from all other iris varieties due to its exceptional vase life.

In Holland, most flower growers use a variety called *Blue Magic*. The bulbs are inexpensive, the variety is easy to grow, and they perform well at high planting densities, even under lower light conditions. But there's one major drawback: the flowers don't open well and have a relatively short vase life. Unfortunately, *Blue Magic's* poor performance at the consumer level contributed to a decline in the reputation of iris overall. Over the past three decades this has been a contributing factor in the crop's diminishing popularity, with iris acreage decreasing by nearly 80% in Holland.

Van der Wereld was a member of a grower group called "Apollo," which specialized in a yellow iris variety with characteristics similar to *Telstar*. Meanwhile, the IVT, a Dutch government-funded institute focused on advancing the development of new varieties introduced a new white iris called *Casa Blanca*. Rooijakkers and van der Wereld among other iris growers joined in a newly formed grower group established to grow this patented variety. IVT went on to develop several other new iris varieties as well. Through these connections, Sun Valley had a front-row seat for testing, introducing, and marketing new iris varieties in the American marketplace.

During the 1980s, Sun Valley had sourced its iris bulbs from bulb exporters in Holland. But after forming the partnership with Rooijakkers and van der Wereld, we began buying directly from the source, right at the heart of bulb production in Holland. We built our own warm rooms and cooling facilities in Arcata, enabling us to take full control of the process. From that point on, we became completely self-sufficient in our iris bulb supply chain.

An iris bulb kept at 87°F will remain completely dormant, and bulbs can be stored at this temperature for up to 12 months. Once the temperature drops to around 65°F, the bulb begins to "wake up," and at 48°F, the activation process accelerates. Often, a combination of 65°F and 48°F treatments is used to prepare the bulbs for planting. In warmer climates, or for summer flowering, a 65°F cooling treatment is typically sufficient to get the bulbs ready.

Having our own warm rooms and cooling rooms allowed us to experiment with different bulb cooling treatment strategies, modifying the strategies to achieve optimum flower quality based on the time of year and growing location. Over the years, I developed specific cooling schedules aimed at producing a plant with not too much foliage, a thick stem, and a large flower. These schedules may have seemed complex or even puzzling to an outsider, but our dedicated team at Sun Valley followed them meticulously, down to the finest detail. The result was a consistently stellar iris that steadily gained market share year after year.

· · ·

Both of my new partners were true visionaries. In their operations in Holland they had already distinguished themselves with bold, forward-thinking ideas. Working with these gentlemen didn't just bring technical expertise, it expanded my own vision and helped shape how I looked at the future.

One moment that's forever etched in my memory happened in 1992. We were planning our first new bulb warehouse of 13,000 square feet. My thinking was cautious; I proposed building just two coolers inside this new building, each encompassing 1,500 square feet. It felt like the responsible thing to do; take it slow and don't overextend.

Jan van der Wereld was sitting in my office, listening carefully. Then he looked at me and said, "Why only two? Why not five?" I remember feeling that knot in my stomach, worried about spending too much too soon. But Jan wasn't deterred. He took an old cigar box, flipped it over, and began scribbling numbers on the back. "How many lily bulbs are we storing in Holland?" he asked. "What are we paying each month in storage fees?"

We ran the numbers together, and it quickly became clear. Building three more coolers wasn't reckless, it was the smart thing to do. They'd pay for themselves in no time. That moment changed the way I looked at growth and risk. We built five coolers in 1992. And the following year, we filled the rest of that 13,000 square-foot warehouse with coolers.

Jacob Rooijakkers (left) and Jan van der Wereld (right)

It was a turning point. A leap of faith backed by vision, trust, and a little bit of math scribbled on the back of a cigar box.

That moment marked more than just an expansion of our cold storage; it marked a shift in mindset. From that point forward, we began operating with clarity and ambition. The foundation had been laid, and the pieces were falling into place. What followed were some of the most rewarding, productive, and impactful years of my journey, years that, looking back, truly earned the title of the next chapter.

Congressman Frank Riggs shovels the official dirt, kicking of the building of the 1992 warehouse.

CHAPTER 9

THE GOLDEN YEARS

It is wonderful how much may be done if we are always doing.

THOMAS JEFFERSON

In 1994, we reached an important milestone: we paid off the loan from RABO Bank. That same year marked another turning point: we built our first new greenhouse, a 55,000 square-foot structure. Up until then, we had been operating within the 440,000 square feet of greenhouses originally constructed by Melridge in the previous decade. But with growing demand and a clearer sense of direction, we took a careful but confident step forward, building our first greenhouse on our own terms. It was designed specifically for growing freesia. That same year we also expanded our bulb warehouse by another 35,000 square feet, adding space for planting lilies and tulips in crates, along with much-needed additional cooler capacity.

I won't bore you with the year-by-year tally of how many square feet we added in greenhouses, warehouses, and coolers, but let me paint the picture this way: From 1994 to 2000, we were in construction mode every single year. It felt like as soon as one building was finished, we were already breaking ground on the next. By the end of that decade we had added 175,000 square feet of warehouse space, 100,000 square feet of coolers, 800,000 square feet of glass greenhouses, 165,000 square feet of Cravo retractable roof greenhouse, and another 900,000 square feet of plastic hoop houses. The hum of progress was constant.

This wasn't expansion for expansion's sake. It was driven by real demand from an ever-growing number of customers who wanted Sun Valley flowers in their stores, and more of them, more often. It was exciting and encouraging all at once. We were stepping into a new era.

Inside one of the bulb warehouse buildings.

What made it all worthwhile wasn't just the numbers or the buildings, it was seeing our flowers show up in places we'd never imagined. I remember walking into a supermarket in Los Angeles and spotting Sun Valley tulips front and center in the floral department. Another time, a friend sent me a photo from a store in Texas; there were our lilies, proudly displayed. It gave me a quiet sense of pride, not just for myself, but for the whole team back in

Arcata. For the crews in the greenhouses, the harvest teams, the folks packing flowers late into the night. Their fingerprints were on every stem, and now those stems were reaching thousands of miles across the country.

Looking back, those early years weren't just about building greenhouses and expanding production. We were also laying the groundwork for something less tangible but far more enduring, the Sun Valley culture. The way we treated each other, the standards we upheld, and the pride we took in our work slowly began to take root. That culture would become our compass in the years ahead, especially when the storms came. I'll speak more about that later in this book, because in many ways, the culture was the glue that held us together.

Most of the greenhouses we added during that time required both a conditional use permit and a coastal development permit, standard for agricultural construction in Humboldt County. These processes were time-consuming, often stretching the timeline by months. But in 1998, a new planning director took the helm at the County, and when we submitted plans for our next greenhouse he took a different view. He determined that this particular greenhouse qualified as a *"principal use"* and would only require a standard building

Picture taken in 1998

permit. Just like that, the permitting timeline was cut by at least four months, a huge win for us, especially since the greenhouse materials we had ordered from Holland were already on the water, headed our way.

The planning director made an administrative decision that the project was exempt from the California Environmental Quality Act (CEQA), but in an effort to be transparent, he published a notice in the *Times-Standard*, the local newspaper. If no one in the community objected, he would move forward and sign off on the permit.

Lo and behold, on the very last day of the appeal period, the City of Arcata filed an objection. The city maintained the greenhouse project fell within its *"sphere of influence"* and argued that it required a full Environmental Impact Report under CEQA. Suddenly, what had looked like a green light turned into a high-stakes political process. The decision now rested with the Humboldt County Board of Supervisors. A hearing was scheduled for Tuesday, May 26, 1998, the day after Memorial Day.

We knew we couldn't take anything for granted. The week prior we mobilized and called on every local vendor who did business with us and asked them to reach out to their district supervisor. We urged them to show up in person to support the project. We also brought a group of Sun Valley team members to the hearing. As each person arrived, they were handed a bright orange button that read, *I Support Sun Valley.*

By the time the hearing began, the Supervisors' chamber was packed wall-to-wall. Nearly every seat was filled with someone wearing that orange button. It was a powerful show of unity, with business owners and team members all standing together. There were only two exceptions: the Arcata City Manager and Connie Stewart, the Mayor of Arcata at the time. They were the only ones not wearing the button.

When it was my turn to address the board of Supervisors, I began with a light-hearted gesture, I wished Connie a happy birthday. Back then, there was no Facebook to look up such things, but I'd heard someone mention it earlier and decided to lead with it. It broke the tension just a bit. Later, when

Connie gave her presentation, she smiled and thanked me for the flowers she had anonymously received that morning. It brought a touch of cheerfulness and humanity to an otherwise high-stakes meeting.

After laying out our case, our plans, our commitment to the community, and the overwhelming support in the room, the Supervisors took their vote. We received unanimous approval. Even Supervisor John Wooley, who represented the third district including Arcata, and who had previously indicated he would vote against us, cast his vote in favor. It was a moment of great relief and quiet triumph.

. . .

Iris was one of the staple crops at Sun Valley, and as our iris program expanded, so did our need for land. To manage this, we developed a rotation system, returning to the same fields every second or third year by fumigating the soil between plantings. In the 1980s and early 1990s, we relied on a combination of methyl bromide and chloropicrin for fumigation.

These soil fumigants were highly effective. They killed nematodes and weed seeds, but most importantly for us, they controlled Fusarium, a soil-borne fungal disease that could devastate an entire iris crop if left untreated. And it wasn't just iris. The Easter lily bulb growers in Smith River, as well as the U.S. Forest Service tree nursery in McKinleyville, relied on this fumigant too. Trical, a company that specialized in the application of the methyl bromide and chloropicrin mix, typically made their way to the North Coast each September. They arrived with several rigs and completed applications for all of us in a short, coordinated window.

The process involved covering the fields with plastic tarps and injecting the fumigants beneath the surface. Methyl bromide also acted as a carrier, helping to distribute the chloropicrin evenly throughout the soil profile. For flower farmers, Easter lily bulb growers, and nurserymen it was a powerful tool, one that provided a level of disease control that would have been much more difficult to achieve by other means.

But there was a serious downside. Methyl bromide was identified as an ozone-depleting substance, and it quickly became a target of environmental concern. Activist groups began to speak out, including a local organization called *Californians for Alternatives to Toxics* (CATs), led by their executive director, Patty Clary.

There was growing resistance within the local community around the use of methyl bromide, and the concerns were impossible to ignore. I had several direct conversations with Patty. At one point, she organized a meeting in September 1995 at the local hospital in Arcata, gathering more than a dozen doctors in one room.

I attended the meeting alongside a scientist from Trical, the company responsible for applying the fumigants. The discussion quickly dove deep into the science, especially the environmental impact of methyl bromide and its role in ozone layer depletion. It was a tense but respectful exchange, with strong opinions on both sides, yet with a shared recognition of the need for informed dialogue.

The pragmatist side in me listened closely. I understood the concerns raised by the doctors and by Patty. And though we had been operating well within the legal guidelines, I also knew that continuing down the same path could drive a wedge between Sun Valley and the community that we called home. From that point forward, voluntarily and a full decade before methyl bromide was officially banned for soil fumigation in the U.S., we made the decision to stop using it at Sun Valley.

That decision marked a turning point. As a gesture of goodwill and mutual respect, I personally helped fund Patty's trip to Europe in December 1995 so she could attend an international meeting of the *Montreal Protocol*, the global treaty designed to protect the ozone layer. My reconciliatory approach to Patty and her organization was paid back in spades as I will reveal later in this book.

Of course, stepping away from methyl bromide came with new challenges. Without fumigation, we now needed a longer rotation cycle to maintain healthy iris crops. And while the Arcata Bottoms may appear vast and open, the land suitable for early spring iris planting is surprisingly limited. Much of the soil is heavy and stays too wet well into the planting season. Complicating things further, an increasing number of the dairies and cattle farmers in the area had converted to organic operations, making it harder for us to rotate onto their land.

A solution presented itself about two hours north of Arcata, in Smith River, California. A 180-acre farm came up for sale, complete with two houses and several barns. The timing was right, and we quickly agreed on a price. By the fall of 1996, we were planting our first crops of daffodils and iris in this new location.

The soil there was a dream, lighter than in Arcata, a beautiful silty loam shaped by centuries of sediment from the nearby Smith River. In 1998, we added hoop houses to the Smith River farm to support winter iris production, and extended our season.

Jim Johnson, who had served for many years as our field manager in Arcata and prior to that at the farm in Myrtle Point, moved up to Smith River to oversee the operation. He made the farm his own and managed it with great care and skill until his retirement in 2008.

Though it was farther north and closer to the ocean, the Smith River farm experienced slightly warmer summer temperatures than Arcata, a detail that often surprises people. But the geography held the explanation. Just north of the Smith River lies a narrow stretch of land known for growing most of the Easter lily bulbs in the U.S. This area, nestled between the Smith River in California and the Chetco River in Oregon, is often referred to as the *Banana Belt*. Thanks to a unique offshore wind pattern known as the *Chetco Effect*, summers there are warmer than in the rest of the Northern California and Oregon coastline. Our farm sat just south of the Smith River, outside the core zone of the effect. It wasn't dramatic, but it allowed us to grow great crops in a region that quickly became an important part of our operation.

• • •

In 1998, one of our sales reps shared that she was repeatedly hearing from customers requesting "Oregon-type" products, things such as Snowberries, Ilex, Rosehips, and a variety of foliage crops. One customer told her, *"We love the Sun Valley quality, and it would be great to see that same standard applied to those berry and foliage crops."*

The coastal climate of Arcata, however, doesn't lend itself to growing these types of products. So, we set out on an exploration mission inland, looking for the closest location near Arcata that might be suitable. That search led us to Willow Creek, a small town about 45 minutes east along State Highway 299. Nestled in a valley carved by the Trinity River, Willow Creek not only had the right climate but also plenty of local charm. It's famously known for its "Bigfoot" memorabilia and the Bigfoot Museum, all stemming from the alleged 1958 Bigfoot sightings in the area.

The climate in Willow Creek is drastically different from the cool, coastal conditions of Arcata. Summer temperatures in Willow Creek regularly climb into the 90s, and it's not unusual to break the 100-degree mark. In winter, temperatures can dip into the low 20s or even the upper teens, much colder than what we typically experience in Arcata. In many ways, the climate in Willow Creek mirrors that of Oregon, where many foliage and berry crops thrive, with one notable advantage, as Willow Creek enjoys a higher annual amount of sunlight hours.

Before we embarked on our exploration mission in November 1998, we had spoken with a local farmer in Willow Creek who was growing peaches and chili peppers. He told us about a nearby farm that had been abandoned for 20 years and was now overgrown with blackberries. That caught our attention.

Because Willow Creek sits in a narrow valley flanked by tall mountain ranges on both sides, we came prepared with a device to measure sunlight exposure, specifically, the hours of direct sun versus shade throughout the day and across seasons. When scouting farmland in a place like the Trinity Valley, this kind of information is critical. The steep hillsides can cast long shadows, and the viability of growing sun-loving crops depends heavily on how much sunlight actually reaches the fields

Our first stop was the abandoned farm we had heard about. Right away, we could see the soil was beautiful, loamy and soft, with no evidence of rocks. The owner told us that the land used to be a lakebed, likely an ancient overflow from the Trinity River. That made sense, especially considering the property now sits about 80 feet above the river. The topsoil went down at least 12 feet, which supported the lakebed theory and spoke volumes about the richness of the land.

We pulled out our sunlight measuring device and found there was a bit of early morning shade, but nothing significant. The property had been untouched for two decades, and it showed. Blackberry bushes had grown wild, some reaching 15 feet tall. Evidence of bear activity was everywhere, with piles of dung scattered throughout. It was clear this place would take a lot of work to clear and reclaim, but it checked all the qualifications we were looking for.

We also looked at a farm closer to Hoopa, the Indian reservation about 10 miles north of Willow Creek, but the soil there was heavy clay mixed with rocks, hard and unforgiving. Other spots we visited were either too small or didn't suit our needs.

After considering all the options, we chose the abandoned property. It was known locally as the Shore Ranch. We negotiated with the owner and agreed on a 10-year lease, with an option to renew it for another 10 years.

A week later, a massive storm hit Northern California, dumping seven inches of rain in Arcata in just 24 hours and causing major local flooding. The day after the storm, I hopped into my pickup truck and headed out to Willow Creek. I wanted to see firsthand how the field we liked so much had handled that kind of rainfall.

I couldn't believe my eyes. As I walked the field and poked around with my shovel, I found hardly any wet spots or puddles. The soil practically fell off the shovel; it was as if it had barely rained. Bewildered, I stopped at the local gas station on my way out of town and asked the lady at the counter, "Did you have any rain yesterday?" She looked at me and said, "Are you kidding? We had nine inches. It was crazy!"

That moment confirmed we had made the right decision. Not only did this field have deep topsoil, but it also drained incredibly well.

The following week, we were out there with a large mower, chopping down the overgrown blackberry bushes. It took us weeks to pull out the roots using a heavy harrow. But by May 1999, the ground was finally in a tillable condition. That first year we planted annuals such as ornamental peppers, grasses such as millet and wheat, sunflowers, and Brain Celosia. We also put in a few perennials, Sedum, Spirea, Lysimachia, and Solidago.

The first Ilex went into the ground a year later, in 2000. We had found a supplier in Boskoop, Holland, who sold us *Oosterwijk* Ilex, the main red variety being grown in Holland at the time. But as it turned out, what we received was actually a mix of different varieties. We later learned that propagating Ilex is not a simple process. Some traders sell Ilex propagated from seed, which is far less uniform.

Years later, what seemed like a calamity at the time ended up becoming a blessing, but I'll explain more about that in a chapter titled the Spirit Ilex Journey.

In those early years, we trialed close to 40 different crops at Willow Creek. We experimented with other shrubs such as Forsythia, Ligustrum berries, and Physocarpus, and perennials such as Echinops, Centaurea, and Echinacea. That same year, 2000, we also planted our first Cotinus. We split the planting; half went into the ground in Arcata and the other half in Willow Creek.

By the fall, the difference was striking. The Cotinus in Arcata had reached about 24 inches in height, while the ones in Willow Creek were over six feet tall. But even more interesting was what happened after harvest. The stems picked in Arcata wouldn't hold up, even when placed in water. In contrast, the Willow Creek stems had excellent vase life.

My thesis was this: the Cotinus in Arcata developed a much denser cell structure due to the cool coastal climate, limiting capillary function. Meanwhile, the higher summer temperatures in Willow Creek allowed the plants to develop cell structures better suited for water uptake, translating into a far better vase life.

That was both the first and last year we grew Cotinus in Arcata. We dug up all the plants and moved them to Willow Creek. Over the years, we continued to expand our plantings, and today, Cotinus is one of the cornerstones of the Willow Creek program.

. . . .

In addition to the Willow Creek expansion, 1999 also brought a significant development right next door to our Arcata farm. Simpson Timber Company, a major landowner in Northern California, had built a series of lumber mills throughout the region during the 1950s. One of those mills, a massive 400,000-square-foot facility, sat on a 200-acre parcel adjacent to our farm.

The mill had been shuttered since the early 1990s, and Simpson was evaluating options for what to do with the idle property. It was listed for sale at $3.1 million. At the same time, Simpson was in discussions with the City of Arcata about annexing the land and converting it into a large residential development.

That idea met with considerable resistance from the local community. Personally, I wasn't too thrilled either. The prospect of a massive housing project going in right next to our farm was a concern to us, not just about land use compatibility, but also the potential impact on our farming operations.

KINS, a local talk radio station, used to run a daily "Question of the Day," where listeners could call one number to vote "yes" and another to vote "no" on a particular topic. In the summer of 1996, they posed a timely question: *Do you agree with the City of Arcata annexing the Simpson property for a housing development?* The station shared the two phone numbers with the audience and let the community weigh in.

By the end of the day, they announced the results. The response was overwhelmingly against the proposal, with, as I recall, around 80% of callers voicing disapproval. I'm not sure if the station tracked who was calling and how many times, but I'll admit that I had the "no" number saved on autodial. I made sure our opinion was heard!

Then, almost magically, within a week, Simpson Timber sent a letter to the Arcata City Council formally withdrawing its plans for the housing development.

Within a month I reached out to the former general manager of the Simpson Mill. At the time, he was semi-retired but still acted as the facility manager for the vacant property. I knew him fairly well as we were both members of the Arcata Rotary Club, so there was already a sense of familiarity. We arranged to meet at the mill site, and I brought along our attorney, Dave Dun. We had a short meeting in his office.

I told him we might be interested in purchasing the property. He handed me a glossy brochure listing the price at $3.1 million. I told him, frankly, that we weren't interested at that price. He encouraged me to give it some thought.

One of my major concerns was the property's history as a lumber mill. Many mills in the area had used pentachlorophenol, a wood preservative later identified as a dangerous carcinogen. I raised this concern, and he quickly reassured us. This mill, he explained, had processed redwood, not Douglas fir. Penta was typically used for fir, which needed the chemical treatment for durability. Redwood, being naturally semi-rot-resistant, didn't require it. That explanation made sense to us, and it put our minds at ease.

The following week, we submitted an offer: $1.3 million in cash, with a three-day window for a response. That Monday, I received a call from the president of Simpson Timber's Northern California division; our offer was accepted.

With that, the due diligence period began. I still had lingering concerns about potential environmental issues on the site, given its long history as a lumber mill. Simpson provided a Phase I environmental study that had been previously commissioned for the City of Arcata as part of its housing development plan. The report, prepared by local engineering firm SHN, appeared generally clean, aside from some minor hydrocarbon issues near the old fuel tanks.

Even so, I wasn't at ease taking on a property with such an industrial past. Someone recommended I contact Linda Mackey at Environet in Santa Rosa. She had a reputation for being thorough and was well-versed in navigating the regulatory landscape. Linda conducted a more in-depth environmental investigation and successfully persuaded Simpson to enter into a voluntary agreement with the California Department of Toxic Substances Control (DTSC). This agreement provided regulatory oversight without a punitive approach, providing an important layer of protection.

Linda brought in a drill rig and collected 120 samples from around the property. Someone from the community had specifically suggested we test under the old lunchroom on the west side of the property, so we did, and it came back completely clean. Linda's team confirmed the same minor hydrocarbon issues noted in the Phase I study, but beyond that, nothing of concern was found.

By this point, I was starting to feel more comfortable, but for some reason, I kept procrastinating on finalizing the due diligence period and closing the transaction with Simpson. I remember Jacob Rooijakkers telling me, *"What are you waiting for, Lane? Just close the deal and get it done."*

By what felt in retrospect like divine intervention, I got a call from Kevin Hoover, editor of the *Arcata Eye* newspaper. The *Arcata Eye* was still in its early days, and I knew Kevin fairly well, his daughter went to the same school as our kids, and we'd been to the same birthday parties. When Kevin had launched the paper he had asked if I'd be willing to lend him $5,000 to get started. I agreed, and he paid the loan back on time. We had a good relationship.

When Kevin called, he said he'd heard rumors that Sun Valley was buying the Simpson property. I told him I couldn't comment, as I wished not to upset a very sensitive negotiation process.

Next thing I know, in the February 11, 1997, issue of the *Arcata Eye* there was a front-page article headlined: **Sun Valley set to buy Simpson land**. Kevin had done his homework, interviewing several people for the article, including Patty Clary, the executive director of Californians for Alternatives to Toxics. In the piece, she was quoted as saying, *"Sun Valley could be buying into a toxic nightmare."* She continued, *"Lane may be buying a Superfund site."* This was shocking news, especially in light of everything we had learned up to that point.

Arcata Eye article February 1997

After reading the article, I picked up the phone and called Patty Clary right away. *"What are you talking about?"* I asked. *"The City of Arcata commissioned a Phase I environmental study, and it came up relatively clean. We're also in the middle of our own investigation through Environet, and so far, there's been no cause for concern."*

She responded, *"Come to my office, I have some information you might want to see."*

Within ten minutes, I was there. She handed me two large boxes filled with court documents from a lawsuit of a former Simpson employee, *Skaggs v. Champion International*, filed against the manufacturer of a chemical product called "Woodlife Clear RTU." The documents detailed cancer-related cases and deaths allegedly linked to the use of pentachlorophenol (Penta), a known carcinogen.

I took the boxes home and started reading. I couldn't put the documents down and read late into the night. I was stunned by the level of detail in the depositions. One described the exact location of a Penta dip tank inside the main building. Another revealed that Penta had been used on the paint line to treat redwood siding. After application, the Penta would cause the wood to "bloom," enhancing the visual effect of the paint job.

The court documents revealed even more disturbing details. The painting line, it turned out, was cleaned every Friday. The leftover sludge, a mix of Penta-laced paint chunks, was dumped just outside the door into a hole that had been dug specifically for that purpose on the south side of the building. Later, after this practice was discontinued, a concrete slab was poured over the site, and a lunchroom was built right on top of it.

That meant the lunchroom we had tested, on the west side, wasn't the one. The real contamination site was under the lunchroom on the *south* side of the building.

The next morning, I called Linda Mackey with this disturbing new information. She immediately notified the California Department of Toxic Substances Control (DTSC), since the site was already under their legal oversight. I also reached out to the team at Simpson. They were clearly caught off guard and a bit sheepish about the revelation. Had this not been under DTSC jurisdiction, they very likely could have backed away from the sale entirely. But with DTSC now fully engaged, Simpson had no choice but to cooperate and allow for a proper cleanup of the site.

The first cleanup project was the lunchroom on the south side, the very one built over the old dumping pit. It came down in less than 30 minutes, leveled by a large excavator. Next, the concrete slab was torn up and then came the real task: excavating nearly 4,000 yards of contaminated soil. As I stood there watching, I could see chunks of paint mixed in the soil, and there was a strange, sweet odor in the air.

The excavated soil was temporarily stored inside the building and later trucked to a certified toxic waste facility in the San Joaquin Valley. Eventually, regulatory oversight of the site was transferred to the North Coast Regional Water Quality Control Board (NCRWQCB). Since 2000, they've conducted quarterly groundwater testing at monitoring wells surrounding the former lunchroom site. That testing continued for over two decades, and on April 26, 2023, the Water Board officially issued a case closure letter, formally concluding their environmental oversight.

The cleanup took more than two years. By the time it was all finished, Simpson had spent $2.1 million on remediation efforts. I had a meeting with the regional president of Simpson, who candidly acknowledged that the cleanup costs had far exceeded the property's $1.3 million purchase price. Still, he told me that with the site now environmentally certified and in much better condition, Simpson could likely sell it at a higher price if they chose to. But to their credit, Simpson's leadership had made the decision to honor our original agreement. Escrow closed on May 7, 1999.

The property itself included 40 acres of asphalt on which lumber had been stacked to dry. To make the land usable, we partnered with a local gravel company. They brought in a massive grinder and began removing the asphalt from 20 acres. Underneath the asphalt there was a layer, two to four feet, of river-run gravel, originally trucked in during the 1950s to support the heavy stacks of drying lumber.

We sold the gravel to the gravel company, and in doing so, began the process of returning the land back to its original state. But it would take more than that to make it viable farmland. The soil beneath had been sealed off and deprived of oxygen for nearly five decades. When first uncovered the soil gave off a sour, almost rotten smell.

We got to work applying lime and planting a series of cover crops over several years to restore the soil's health. Slowly but surely, the former Simpson mill site was ready, transformed into productive, arable farmland.

The property also came with a commodious office building, which turned out to be a great asset. With our growing administrative and sales staff, we began using the new office space in 2000.

Initially, we didn't have much use for the massive 400,000-square-foot mill building, but in the ensuing years as our tulip program continued to expand, we began constructing coolers inside to support that growth. The paved areas where we hadn't removed the asphalt also proved useful for soil operations, particularly for storing and processing composted bark, the primary growing medium for our tulip and Oriental lily programs.

Looking back, 1999 was truly a momentous year for Sun Valley. In addition to purchasing the Simpson property, we also acquired a ranch in Willow Creek. That same year, we built 170,000 square feet of glass greenhouses, 200,000 square feet of hoophouses, added 22,000 square feet of warehouse space, and 18,000 square feet of cold storage. What's perhaps most remarkable is that all of this, every square foot, was paid for entirely from the business's own cash flow.

. . .

At the onset of our tulip program in the 1980s we used a soil mixture that was predominantly based on peat moss. Initially, we purchased bagged peat moss from Canada. Shortly thereafter, we discovered a local source, a man who operated a peat bog in the mountains near Bridgeville, California. We used his material throughout the remainder of the decade and into the early nineties. Because tulips are particularly susceptible to soil-borne pathogens like *Pythium* (root rot) and *Phytophthora* (soft rot), our soil supplier incorporated several fungicides into the mix to help mitigate these threats.

A major breakthrough came in 1992 when I received a call from a fellow who had been hired by Sierra Pacific Industries to clean up their log yard. Over the years, bark that had been peeled off from the logs had mixed with the underlying gravel and rocks in their log yard. Each summer, when the ground was dry enough, this debris had been pushed aside, eventually forming a pile estimated at over 50,000 yards. This man operated a clever machine that screened the material, separating the bark from the rocks. The bark chunks were sold to the local cogeneration power plant as fuel, while the rocks were sold to gravel companies. What remained was the by-product known as the fines, a mix of partially composted bark, silt, and small rock particles less than an inch in size.

We planted some crates of tulips and lilies in this soil, and to our pleasant surprise, both crops performed better than those grown in the traditional peat moss mix. The results were clear; this newly discovered medium was not only cost-effective but also grew superior crops.

Sierra Pacific was glad to have the fines removed from their property, and at the time, all we paid was the cost of trucking. Since their lumber mill was just three miles from the farm, we suddenly had access to a steady supply of high-quality soil at a very attractive price.

Even more remarkable, we soon discovered that we no longer needed to mix fungicides into our soil blend. The composting process of the bark had created high levels of beneficial microorganisms, which, combined with the excellent drainage of the fines, produced a growing medium so robust that chemical control was no longer necessary. It truly was a game changer.

It took several years to use up the fines from the Sierra Pacific site, so we soon began sourcing similar material from other old mill sites in the region. We tapped into the Blue Lake Forest Products mill near Blue Lake, the Simpson mill in Korbel, the Pacific Lumber sites in Carlotta and Scotia, and even an old mill site in Fields Landing.

As time went on, the cost of this soil gradually increased. Trucking from more distant locations added to the expense, and the mills eventually realized that this by-product had value to us. But for the next 30 years, this unique soil became the foundation of Sun Valley's tulip and Oriental lily programs.

One key lesson we learned over the years was how critical the type of logs processed at each mill site could be. The best-performing soil came from bark sourced from Douglas fir, Grand fir, White fir, or Spruce logs. In contrast, Redwood bark was less desirable. Once dried, Redwood-based soil had a tendency to resist rehydration, making it harder to manage. In cases where

Redwood fines were present, we used them sparingly, blending them carefully with other material to avoid compromising the mix.

A close-up of the soil operations at the old Simpson property.

The Arcata Greenhouses and in the left top corner, the 400,000 square-foot Simpson building. The soil operations were situated between the greenhouses and the Simpson building. Picture taken in 2007.

. . .

On the home front, things were progressing well. My wife and I had purchased a wooded lot about eight minutes from the farm, on a hill in McKinleyville. It had a perfect view overlooking the Arcata Bottoms and the farm itself. We hired a logger to clear just enough trees to create a building site for what we envisioned would one day be our dream home. The plan was to start small, with a 24-foot-by-36-foot barn-style cabin and live there for a while before building our dream home.

The prefab kit arrived with what seemed like hundreds of components. A building contractor poured the foundation, but from there my wife and I took on the construction ourselves, helped by a handyman from the farm. We spent many weekends hammering, lifting, and learning. By the summer of 1992, we had built a place we proudly called our own home.

After enduring the emotional pain of several miscarriages, my wife and I made the decision to adopt. In November 1993, Tony was born, and we brought him home the very next day from the hospital. Two years later, in January 1996, Sarah was born at the same hospital. With a boy and a girl, the DeVries family had doubled in size, and our lives were enriched beyond anything we had ever imagined.

These kids grew up with the farm. They often accompanied me on weekly trips to Del Norte and Willow Creek. One especially memorable moment came in April 1999, when I took Tony to the WFFSA (flower wholesalers) convention in Monterey. There were two days of grower tours, and Tony, then just five years old had a great time riding the buses and mingling with folks on the tours. Even today, people in the industry still ask me how Tony is doing. They remember that energetic, entertaining little guy from that convention.

CHAPTER 10

SPREADING OUR WINGS

*Great effort springs naturally from a great attitude, excellence
is the gradual result of always striving to do better. There are
only two options regarding commitment. You're either IN
or you're OUT. There is no such thing as life in-between.*

PAT RILEY

The late 1990s saw a wave of major consolidation in the floral industry. One of the most notable was the formation of *USA Floral Products Inc.* in 1997. That involved a merger of 14 floral companies, including The Roy Houff Company, Bay State Florist Supply Inc., United Wholesale Florists Inc., Johnson Roses, Monterey Bay Bouquet Inc., Alpine Gem Flower Shippers Inc., XL Group Inc., Koehler and Dramm Inc., Atlantic Bouquet Ltd., CFX Inc., Continental Farms Ltd., Everflora Inc., Flower Trading Corporation, La Fleurette, and UltraFlora Corporation. The company moved aggressively, acquiring additional floral firms, and after its acquisition of Florimex, it surpassed $1 billion in annual revenues.

Around the same time, Dole Food Company entered the floral business in a big way. In 1998, it acquired a major Colombian flower grower Florimérica

, along with Sunburst Farms, its distribution arm in the U.S., followed by adding Finesse Farms, CCI Farms, and Four Farmers Inc. to their portfolio. In other words, as the millennium approached, the floral industry was in the midst of a serious M&A boom.

That August, John Tate, CFO of Dole, paid a visit to our farm in Arcata. All this activity in the industry stirred something in me. We had, by every indicator, a successful company, one with strong financials and profit margins that outperformed many of the businesses being absorbed by these emerging floral conglomerates. It started to give me an itch.

In the seven years following the acquisition of the company in 1991, we had established strong market recognition with our core crops, lilies, tulips, and iris. The company was not only profitable but also growing rapidly. It is no understatement to say that by 1998 we had become a recognized name in the industry.

That summer, we had a conversation with Bob Poirier, CEO of USA Floral. He visited Arcata in July 1998 to explore a possible acquisition. But I wasn't interested in selling the company for USA Floral stock. My ambition reached farther, and it was fueled by a deeper sense of purpose: I wanted to bring in private equity to help propel Sun Valley's growth as a stand-alone platform company, one that could make its own acquisitions and chart its own course.

In August 1998, I attended a seminar organized by Geneva, a boutique M&A firm focused on small- to mid-market companies. Their presentation resonated with me, and by October we had formally engaged Geneva to represent us. They developed a professional prospectus for potential investors, and the response was overwhelming. We received 15 offers from private equity firms eager to invest in Sun Valley, without even having visited the company.

By the summer of 1999, we narrowed that list to five finalists, inviting them to Arcata for face-to-face meetings, with my Dutch partners in attendance. After careful consideration, KRG Capital Partners from Denver, Colorado, emerged as the right fit.

Due diligence took some time, but by June 2000, we finalized the deal, selling 40% of the company to KRG. Together, we laid out ambitious plans to grow Sun Valley through strategic acquisitions.

Shortly after the deal closed, we hit the ground running. Alongside a few of the KRG partners, we began visiting potential acquisition targets in Southern California. Our first stop was Pleasant Valley Flowers, owned by Wim Zwinkels, a longtime friend and respected grower. Wim's operation focused on crops well-suited to the Southern California climate: Matsumoto Aster, Bella Donna Delphinium, Larkspur, and Lisianthus. He also grew lilies, as well as a few tulips and iris.

Wim was 58 at the time and ready to sell his business. Pleasant Valley Flowers had been doing okay. But he was selling his lilies at a lower price than we were at Sun Valley, while paying more for his bulbs, a clear indicator that there was room for operational improvement. On August 1, 2001, we finalized the deal, and overnight, our product offerings expanded to include a range of crops well-suited to the Southern California climate.

Just a few weeks later, I received a call from Gary Miller, owner of Golden Coast Greenhouses, located less than a mile from Pleasant Valley. He informed me that he was preparing to file for Chapter 11 bankruptcy and wanted to know if we were interested in participating in a Section 363 sale, acting as the stalking horse bidder at a predetermined price. The deal would include crop inventory, customer lists, the Golden Coast tradename, and equipment.

Golden Coast Greenhouses was well known in the industry for its Gerberas and Oriental lilies, especially the variety *Starfighter*. We reached an equitable purchase agreement, but it still required approval from the Bankruptcy Court in Santa Barbara.

At the hearing, another flower grower stepped forward with interest in the purchase. But the judge, clearly not wanting to drag the process out, insisted the transaction be closed that day. We were ready. By the time we walked out of the courtroom, Golden Coast was officially part of the Sun Valley Group.

Initially, we leased the Golden Coast property for three years, and in 2004 we purchased it from Gary Miller. These two acquisitions in Oxnard significantly transformed Sun Valley. We were no longer just the "bulb flower company" we had been known as for decades. The expanded crop portfolio not only diversified our offerings but also helped solidify the bouquet business, which had been steadily growing.

. . .

The list of customers wanting to carry Sun Valley tulips kept growing steadily. At the time, Kroger was already buying our tulips for California and Colorado divisions, but for their main divisions, NFC and SFC, they were still sourcing Dutch-grown tulips.

I remember visiting the Kroger buying office in Vero Beach, Florida, in the summer of 1999. We made our case: put Sun Valley tulips side by side with the Dutch imports and let the consumer decide. The buyer seemed receptive and asked us to provide a quote for their main divisions. On the way back to the airport, we worked up the numbers in real time, coordinating with the team in Arcata. Before we even boarded the plane home, the quote was sitting on the Kroger buyer's desk.

Tulips in the Arcata Greenhouse

The next day, we got the call. *"We don't just want to try a small portion of our program with your tulips; we want you to do the whole thing."*

That single decision had a massive ripple effect. It meant we had to buy significantly more bulbs and urgently expand the cooler space to support the increase in volume.

Over the next few years, demand for Sun Valley tulips only grew stronger. Central Market and HEB signed on to carry Sun Valley tulips, followed by multiple divisions of Whole Foods, Sprouts, and Trader Joes. Then came a major milestone, every SAM's Club location nationwide began offering our tulips. Eventually, even Walmart came knocking, based on the strong results it had observed from the SAM's Club program.

Initially, Walmart awarded us eight regional divisions. Encouraged by the performance and consistency of our tulips, they expanded the partnership the following season, granting us the opportunity to supply the entire Walmart U.S. footprint.

1-800-Flowers started with modest volumes in our first year of doing business together. At the time, we were just one of several suppliers, and it wasn't clear where the relationship would go. But we focused on what we did best: growing beautiful, dependable tulips and delivering them on time, every time.

Over the years, as we proved ourselves season after season, the relationship deepened. Trust grew, and the volumes steadily increased. It wasn't long before our tulips became a core part of their spring floral program. Eventually, Sun Valley became the primary supplier for 1-800-Flowers' tulip offerings, covering an incredible 95% of their needs.

What set us apart wasn't just the product, it was our consistency and commitment to quality. 1-800-Flowers understood that their customers expected something special, and they knew that cutting corners wasn't worth the cost. They were willing to pay for quality, and we were proud to deliver it.

Looking back, that partnership reinforced a lesson I had learned time and again: real growth doesn't come from shortcuts. It comes from relationships built on trust, and from doing the hard work, quietly, consistently, and with purpose.

In the spring of 1999, even Martha Stewart came to visit the farm in Arcata. Her influence on home and garden trends was and still is immense, and she wanted to see firsthand what was happening at Sun Valley, especially our tulip program. We gave her a full tour of the operation, and I drove her around in my pickup truck.

She was curious, hands-on, and asked thoughtful questions about our growing practices, harvesting techniques, and the logistics behind getting fresh flowers from field to consumer. She took particular interest in the quality and consistency of our tulips, which were in full production during her visit. It was a memorable day, not only because of who she was, but because of the genuine interest and respect she showed for the work we were doing.

Martha Stewart visit in 1999

In the years that followed, while her direct-to-consumer website was active, we packed and shipped tulips and other crops for her brand. It was a rewarding collaboration that helped showcase our tulips and other flowers.

As the tulip program continued to expand in Arcata, we had to real-locate greenhouse space to keep up. We made room by moving our Oriental lily production from Arcata to Oxnard. At its peak, Sun Valley was growing more than 120 million tulips a year. Visitors often asked how many we grew, but I never gave a straight answer. I didn't want it to come off as bragging, and besides, it was more fun to keep everyone guessing. Now that the company is no longer in business, I feel more at ease sharing some of the numbers, not to boast, but to offer perspective for the reader.

In the early 2000s, all of our tulips were still grown in soil. That system required significant cooler capacity since the bulbs were all planted in the fall through mid-January, then rooted and stored at 29°F until they were brought into the greenhouse. The newly acquired Simpson building turned out to be a key asset. We converted more than 45,000 square feet into dedicated cooler space, essential for our expanding program. A portion of that large, cold building was also used in winter months for rooting both tulips and Oriental lilies.

• • •

At Pleasant Valley, iris had only been a small crop, but we quickly discovered that iris performed exceptionally well in Oxnard during the winter months. Meanwhile, demand for Sun Valley iris continued to grow, and winter hoop-house space in Arcata was limited. As a result, most of the growth in our iris program, especially for the major floral holidays, shifted to Oxnard.

Iris in one of the fields in Oxnard

Over the next decade, iris became the largest crop in Oxnard. At its peak, Sun Valley was growing more than 60 million iris annually. The dominant variety was *Telstar* and made Sun Valley the largest customer of the Telstar group. With the volumes we were purchasing, we gained the leverage to negotiate more favorable pricing for their bulbs. Our position in the Iris market only grew stronger over time. Eventually, Sun Valley captured an 85% market share for iris in the U.S.

. . .

Royal lilies remained a vital part of our product lineup. At the height of production, Sun Valley grew more than 18 million Royals annually, shipping them to customers all across the country. For the winter and early spring months, mid-December through March, all Royal production came from our farm in Oxnard, as the temperatures in Arcata were simply too low for optimal growth. From April through mid-December, however, production shifted to Arcata, where the Royals were grown in hoophouses.

In the summer months especially, the quality of the Arcata-grown lilies consistently outperformed those from Southern California. That's why we implemented a four-month summer break in Oxnard, allowing Arcata to take the lead during the warm season when its conditions yielded the best quality.

Prior to 2001, Stargazer was the primary Oriental lily variety we grew at Sun Valley. That changed after our acquisition of Golden Coast, where we discovered they were growing a variety called Starfighter, hybridized and owned by Sande BV in Holland. Once we began operating the Golden Coast facility and working with Starfighter, we quickly realized that, although it was slightly slower-growing in the greenhouse, it outperformed Stargazer during the winter months. It was also not prone to leaf scorch in the larger sizes, which was a significant issue with Stargazer.

After discussing this with Jacob Rooijakkers, I suggested to him to inquire if he could purchase the variety rights from Sande BV. He did, and this move made Rooijakkers the largest Starfighter grower in Holland virtually overnight, and at the same time, it secured a reliable supply of this exceptional variety for Sun Valley. Within just a few years, we phased out Stargazer from our assortment, and Starfighter became the dominant Oriental lily in our offering for many years to come.

As the demand for greenhouse space for tulips in Arcata increased, more Oriental lily production shifted to Oxnard, particularly during the winter months to meet Valentine's Day and Mother's Day demand peaks. Oriental lilies remained a core product for Sun Valley, where we grew more than 22 million of these lilies annually at our peak. Sun Valley was one of the first growers in the U.S. to introduce double lilies in 2009. Although the program was slow to gain traction initially, it eventually found its place in the market and grew in popularity.

• • •

One of the first things we did after acquiring the Oxnard location was to make plans to expand the warehouse square footage. We needed more cold storage capacity and a temperature-controlled facility to process flowers harvested from both Pleasant Valley and Golden Coast. To put things in perspective: Golden Coast had 600,000 square feet of greenhouse space with just 7,000 square feet of warehouse, and Pleasant Valley had 500,000 square feet of greenhouses, 60 acres of field and hoop production, and only 8,000 square feet of warehouse. These ratios were typical of many California flower farms at the time, but they also reflected a common shortfall in post-harvest investment.

In 2003, our expansion was completed: 33,000 additional square feet, including 12,000 square feet of mezzanine space for cardboard storage, 18,000 square feet of cooler space, and five loading docks. Yet with the growth that followed, even this space was not enough. We eventually moved our bouquet operations into a newly constructed cooler behind the main warehouse. And during peak holiday periods, we coordinated with local produce companies for offsite cross-docking, whatever it took to keep up with demand.

Sales built steadily year after year, eventually pushing annual revenues past the equivalent of $148 million in today's dollars. In California, the largest floral-producing state in the country, more than 32% of the state flower production value came from Sun Valley's greenhouses and fields. We weren't just part of the industry anymore; we were helping to shape it.

But it wasn't just about the scale. Every step, from expanding cooler space to reorganizing workflows, was grounded in something deeper: our pursuit of purpose. We weren't simply trying to grow bigger, our goal was striving to grow *better*, to raise the bar for quality, consistency, and reliability in the flower industry. That commitment drove every investment and every decision.

In 2006, we bought the shares back from KRG with much confidence in the future. Looking back, the period from 1991 to 2008 was one of growth, prosperity, and expanding recognition of both the Sun Valley flowers and the Sun Valley brand. Our reach broadened and our infrastructure matured.

By the end of 2007, we had no idea what was about to unfold in the year ahead, but the events of 2008 would test that pursuit of purpose like never before and ultimately reshape the path forward.

CHAPTER 11

BACK PAIN EXPERIENCE

In reading the lives of great men, I found that the first victory they won was over themselves... self-discipline with all of them came first.

HARRY TRUMAN

In the spring of 2007, I began experiencing persistent pain in my back, along with frequent spasms that made it hard to stand up straight, especially in the mornings or after sitting at my desk. Lying flat on my back for a few minutes and taking some Advil would usually help the pain subside. But by summer, things took a turn.

One day, I was riding my bicycle up a steep hill, pushing hard on the pedals. The moment I got off the bike, a sharp, radiating pain shot from my lower back down into my legs. This time, Advil didn't help and lying flat on the floor didn't help. Nothing helped.

After several painful days with no improvement, I turned to the internet and came across a site called *LoseTheBackPain.com*. I ordered their instructional video, hoping for relief, but the pain was so intense, I couldn't even perform the exercises.

Eventually, I saw a doctor. He ordered an MRI and referred me to physical therapy. The physical therapist gave me an electrotherapy TENS unit, a small device that delivered electrical pulses to targeted points on my back. It had a frequency dial, and I would crank it up when the pain became unbearable. It didn't eliminate the pain, but it brought some relief. At night, I lay flat with a pillow under my knees, the TENS unit humming quietly on its lowest setting, and on some of the better nights, I could sleep a few hours.

Walking was nearly impossible, but I refused to let the pain keep me from the farm. The walk from my house to the truck was agonizing, but once I was seated, the pain eased. At the office, sitting at my desk was tolerable, until I needed to get up and walk even a few steps to the bathroom. Still, I wanted to stick to our regular farm tours with the agronomists, three times a week. I found that bending forward on a bicycle eased the pain, so we made the switch, everyone grabbed a bike, and the farm tours continued, just as before. Even the weekly trips to Oxnard went on. Sitting in the airplane was manageable, and once I got to the Oxnard farm, the team had rounded up a few bikes there as well. We didn't miss a beat.

Then came the day of the MRI. I had to remove my "little friend," the TENS unit, and lie down on the table, flat, with no pillow under my knees. The pain was indescribable. The scan lasted nearly an hour, and when it was over, every step I took felt like three knives were stabbing into my shins. The short walk from the MRI room to my truck felt like a marathon. I sat there in the driver's seat, trying to compose myself.

The hospital was only a mile from the farm. When I walked back into the office, I was white as a sheet. Two days later, I had an appointment with the best neurosurgeon in Humboldt County. Once again, the walk from my truck to his office felt endless. I finally sat down, and the surgeon placed the MRI films on the lightbox. As the images lit up, there was no denying it, my back was in serious trouble.

The MRI images made the problem painfully clear, the disc between L4 and L5 had slipped out and was pressing directly against my spinal cord. That explained why standing up straight or lying flat triggered such excruciating pain.

It was 1:30 p.m. on a Friday. The neurosurgeon looked at me gravely and said that under normal circumstances, he would recommend emergency surgery. But he was leaving the next morning for a three-week vacation. Thankfully, he had already contacted St. Joseph's Hospital in Eureka, where an anesthesiologist was standing by to administer an epidural cortisone injection, precisely targeted at the area where the disc had slipped.

He told me, *"Hopefully, this will relieve the pain long enough for us to reassess when I return."*

There was only one problem, he advised me not to drive afterward. My wife had just left for Disneyland with our daughter and two nieces visiting

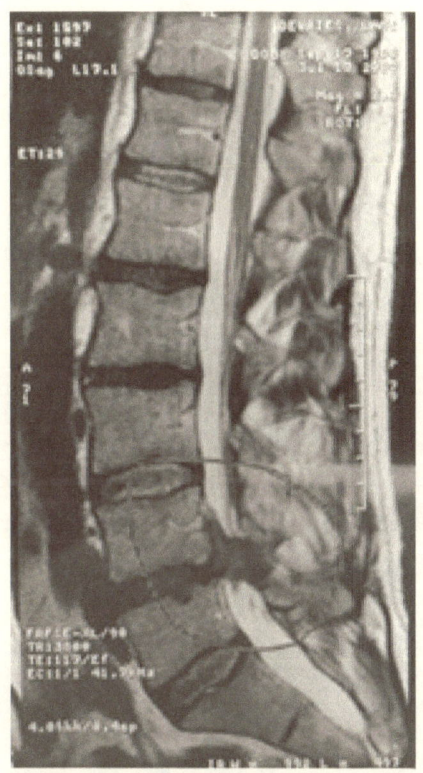

Slipped disk pressing against spinal cord

from Holland. So I asked someone from the farm to drive me to the hospital.

After the epidural, I went home and lay down, for the first time in what felt like forever, I could stretch my legs without pain. Within just a few days, I was walking without the debilitating discomfort that had gripped me for months.

Three weeks later, the neurosurgeon returned. I casually walked into his office, and he could hardly believe his eyes. *"I'm not doing surgery,"* he said. *"Not unless things start to worsen again."* I asked him how my case ranked among others he had seen in his career. He replied, *"Not the worst, but definitely one of the worst."*

From that point on, I followed one simple exercise I had learned from the *Lose the Back Pain* video, lying flat on my back and pulling my knees toward my chest, about 30 repetitions. It takes no more than five minutes, but I've done it every single morning since 2007, no matter where I happen to be. That small act of discipline helps strengthen the core muscles in the abdomen, which in turn reduces strain on the lower back.

Over the years, I've shared that exercise with many others who've suffered from back pain. It's a small gesture, but one rooted in experience, and purpose. That excruciating season of pain became an unexpected blessing. It gave me not only healing, but also a way to help others.

The key is discipline. When the pain is gone, the temptation is to ease up on the routine. But that's when the real risk returns. Staying committed, especially when the urgency is gone, is what matters.

Once again, the Lord had blessed me with a miracle, healing me from a condition that had brought me to my knees. And in doing so, He gave me purpose, not just to endure, but to help others carry their burden.

CHAPTER 12

TROUBLE IN PARADISE

A bend in the road is not the end of the road
unless you fail to make the turn.

HELEN KELLER

I
t may be helpful to provide some background before diving into the story
that forever changed the trajectory of our company.

Back in the 1980s, the Sun Valley team was primarily made up of
local residents, people who had spent most of their lives in Humboldt County,
along with students from Humboldt State University. Harvesting flowers
seven days a week often posed unique challenges, especially on weekends. I
vividly remember the daffodil season, hoping each year that Super Bowl Sunday wouldn't coincide with a warm winter storm. When it did, as it once did,
we were painfully short on daffodil pickers, and we simply couldn't keep up
with the harvest. By the following week, we were snapping off countless open
blooms that had missed their window.

At the time many of the local dairy farmers, as well as the Easter lily growers in Smith River, had already begun employing workers from Mexico. But
at Sun Valley, we were slower to adopt this shift in the workforce. It wasn't

until the late 1980s that a handful of individuals from a single Mexican family joined our team. As the company grew, so did our need for dependable, year-round help. By the 1990s, the Sun Valley workforce had evolved into a diverse mix of local residents, immigrants from Southeast Asia, and workers from Mexico and various Central American countries.

In 2005, we were contacted by a federal agent from the field office of U.S. Immigration and Customs Enforcement (ICE) in Redding, California. He requested a face-to-face meeting with my HR director and me. That summer, we drove to Redding and met with him at his office.

During the meeting, he pointed out that we had a large Hispanic labor force and suggested, somewhat vaguely, that we should make efforts to increase the ratio of Caucasian versus Hispanic workers. At the same time, however, he emphasized that we could not discriminate against Hispanic applicants by scrutinizing their identification documents more closely than others. His guidance boiled down to what he called the "two-feet rule": if a document appeared legitimate when held at a distance of two feet, we were to assume the applicant was legally eligible to work in the United States.

We complied with his request. In the fall of 2005, we went out of our way to hire as many local workers as possible. During the 2005–2006 season, we brought on high school and college students to work on weekends, all in an effort to improve the worker ratio as the ICE agent in Redding had suggested.

The challenge, however, was that the attrition rate among local hires was significantly higher than among our Hispanic workers. Let's face it, agricultural work is not for the faint of heart. It's demanding, with long days and, at times, seven-day work weeks.

Despite our difficulty in maintaining the suggested ratios, the ICE field agent in Redding was satisfied with our efforts. Our HR director had one follow-up meeting with him, and after that, we never heard from him again.

Internally, the conflicting guidance from ICE left us walking a tightrope. On one hand, we were being encouraged, though not officially mandated, to adjust the demographic makeup of our workforce. On the other hand, we were warned not to show any bias in how we verified legal documents. It placed our HR team in a difficult position, trying to strike a balance between compliance, fairness, and operational needs.

Still, we did our best to navigate the situation with integrity. We followed the "two-feet rule" as instructed, avoided over-scrutinizing certain applicants, and documented everything. For a while, things seemed to settle. The agent from Redding had disappeared from the radar, and we continued our focus to growing the company.

But beneath the surface, trouble was brewing.

In November 2007, we received a letter from the San Francisco office of U.S. Immigration and Customs Enforcement, requesting copies of all I-9 employment eligibility forms we had on file. All companies need to keep these forms on file for review, but with the size of our workforce by then, gathering these forms was no small task. We put together four large boxes of documents and sent them off to the ICE office in San Francisco.

After that, we heard nothing, for months.

But in June 2008, everything changed. An ICE agent delivered a letter at the Arcata office. Inside, it stated that 283 team members from our Arcata workforce were believed to have possibly invalid identification documents. The letter noted that anyone who felt ICE's determination was in error should contact their office immediately.

I was stunned. 283 people. That wasn't just a number. These were men and women who worked at Sun Valley every single day. People who were deeply woven into the fabric of our company, some of whom had been with us for close to 20 years, through thick and thin. They were friends, colleagues, and part of the Sun Valley family. But now their livelihoods, and lives, were hanging in the balance.

We knew we had to address this head-on. I called a special farm meeting for Monday, June 9, 2008. That in itself was unusual. Our team was used to regular farm meetings, every four weeks, Fridays in Arcata and Thursdays in Oxnard. These gatherings were part of who we were as a company. They were open, honest, and a space where we shared how the business was doing and celebrated the people behind it. I'll speak more about those meetings in a chapter titled "The Sun Valley Culture."

But this one… was different.

Scheduling a Monday meeting stirred concern even before a single word was spoken. The mood was heavy. People showed up with anxious looks and whispered questions. As I stood before the assembled team, I could feel the weight in the air.

I explained the letter, and the potential consequences. I tried to speak clearly, but my voice was heavy with emotion. The reaction was immediate, astonishment, disbelief, heartbreak. Tears streamed down faces. Some sat frozen in shock.

It was one of the most painful days in our company's history, and for me personally.

What follows is the talk I gave to the team that day, a moment I will never forget, and a turning point in our journey as a company and a community.

JUNE 9 ADDRESS TO
ALL TEAM MEMBERS ARCATA

Dear fellow team members.

When I was 23 years old, I left Holland and came to this country filled with hope and aspiration. I know what it means to leave everything behind and start over, and I deeply sympathize with everyone who has come to this great land to provide for their families.

This country was built by immigrants. In fact, there are likely more immigrants in the United States than in any other nation on earth. For over a century, America has opened its doors to people from around the world, offering not just opportunity, but also dignity and a chance to contribute meaningfully to a shared future.

For the past 25 years, I have loved this country. It has given me the opportunity to grow, to build, and to be part of something greater than myself. But today, I want to be honest with you: I am deeply frustrated and disappointed in our government. The lack of understanding and tolerance toward immigration stands in stark contrast to the values this nation was built upon.

By making it nearly impossible for immigrants to legalize their status, our government is denying prosperity and peace to millions of hard-working people who have come to this great nation in search of a better life. Many of you came here with that very goal, to create a future for yourselves and your families. And most of you have worked at Sun Valley for many years, some nearly 20 years.

This farm could not have grown into what it is today without the dedication, resilience, and hard work of so many of you.

My deepest gratitude goes out to every member of this team for your extraordinary work ethic, your commitment to excellence, and the team spirit you have consistently shown. Together, we have built something special. Sun Valley has a team that is respected and admired across the floral industry, a team I am truly proud of.

We are all aware of the presence of the immigration service, what is now called ICE. For many years, they did not interfere with our operations because we consistently followed the law. That law required us to review identification documents and assess their authenticity to the best of our ability.

About seven months ago, we were instructed to submit all of our I-9 forms for review. Then, just last week, an ICE agent arrived in person to deliver a letter indicating that a significant number of our team members appear to have identification documentation that may not be valid.

At the same time, we've seen case after case across the country where ICE has enforced these laws with full force, including civil and criminal penalties. These measures affect not just individuals with questionable documentation, but also the companies who employ them. It feels as though someone put a loaded revolver at our head, and we're being told what we must do.

Or to use another metaphor: we are flying a small airplane, and a fighter jet has just locked a laser-guided missile onto us, forcing us to land. That's how this situation feels. In other words, what is happening today is not our choice, we are being forced to act on the letter we received from ICE.

I hate every minute of this. It makes me sick to my stomach.

It feels like a bad dream to be standing here in front of you with this news. But I have the misfortune of informing you that the ICE letter indicates the documentation of a significant number of members of this team appears to be incorrect. The consequence, under current law, is that those individuals are not eligible to work in the United States.

There is a chance that mistakes have been made. If you believe there is an error, and you have valid identification, please bring it to our HR department as soon as possible for review.

Everyone will receive a letter today. That letter will indicate whether your name appeared on the ICE list or not. If your letter states that your name did not appear on the list, we ask that you attend a meeting tomorrow morning at 7:30 a.m. at this same location.

Today is a dark day for this company. Saying goodbye is hard in any situation, but given the current circumstances, I am saddened beyond words. I am deeply disillusioned and frustrated with Congress for failing, despite repeated efforts, to pass a lasting solution to the immigration issue.

I am angry that certain companies are being made scapegoats for a national immigration crisis. And now, our company has become one of them. The consequences will be lasting. The heart and soul of our team is being torn out, right here, right now.

And yet, I want you to know this: together, we have conquered mountains. No challenge has ever been too great for this group. You are like family to me. And while it may be hard to do so in this moment, I believe we are being tested, not only in our endurance but in our ability to adapt and carry on.

We must try, as painful as it is, to search for a seed of equivalent benefit within this difficult situation.

Thank you all, from the bottom of my heart.

Usually, our monthly farm meetings were full of excitement and luster, filled with laughter, energy, and a shared sense of purpose. But the meeting in June 2008, was unlike anything I had ever experienced. It was, without question, one of the most somber, anxiety-laden gatherings in the history of our company.

When it ended, the silence was haunting. Some team members just sat there, staring into space, frozen in disbelief. Others wept openly. Many clung to one another in quiet embrace, trying to process what had just unfolded. The feeling in the room was surreal. I had a strong premonition that this moment would mark a turning point in Sun Valley's history.

The months that followed proved that in no uncertain terms.

While many team members were forced to leave, a smaller group received a different kind of letter, one that informed them they had been cleared. But with that clearance came a quiet and heavy responsibility, to pick up the pieces, and to help carry forward the work of so many who were no longer standing beside them. They were not simply survivors. They were now the keepers of our culture, and the bridge between what we had been and what we still hoped to become.

Following is the letter that was shared with those team members, the ones who were asked, in that moment of heartbreak and upheaval, to help hold the line.

> Dear Team Member,
>
> This letter is to inform you that your name was not included on the list provided by the Immigration Service. We are going through a very difficult time as a company, and your continued presence means a great deal.
>
> Since you are part of the team that remains, I ask you to attend an important meeting tomorrow morning at 7:30 a.m. at this same location. During this meeting, we will discuss the future direction of our company and what will be required of us moving forward.
>
> Our group has never faced adversity quite like this. Now more than ever, I ask each of you to work together, step up, and be prepared to do whatever it takes to help carry this company through.
>
> Thank you,
> Lane

The group that was left the next morning amounted to less than half of the original workforce that we had in pace just 24 hours earlier. Following are excerpts of the speech I gave when addressing the remaining team:

Team,

Yesterday was one of the darkest days in the history of our company. Today we turn a new page. The group that is sitting here today has a profound opportunity to help shape the future of this company.

This group will prove that we can beat the odds. We have a huge task ahead of us. Yesterday we lost 283 team members with invaluable experience and knowledge of the operation. Among them a leadership structure that took many years to build.

The team leaders and assistant team leaders of five crews are no longer with us. For the moment we have appointed several team members as acting Team leaders.

Here is the game plan for bringing in new team members

Express personnel is sending 25 people today.

We are going to do radio and TV advertising. A referral bonus is being activated for any team member who brings a new team member who then works for at least 90 days. We encourage part-timers to work flex hours.

We are signing up for an H2A program to bring seasonal team members to the farm for a period that cannot exceed nine months.

It is important that we continue to follow our guiding principles.

Folks, here we are on this new day. We will rise from the ashes of yesterday's devastation with new vigor. We will enter this new chapter and go through it together. And ultimately our team will come back on top and be stronger than ever.

The game plan we laid out during that meeting was largely implemented as discussed. It coincided with the first week of summer vacation for local high school students. We reached out to the four largest high schools in Humboldt County, and they helped spread the word to students on summer break. This gave us a sizable influx of new workers.

Training unskilled folks to pick flowers at the ideal harvest stage proved to be a real challenge. Knowing which flowers are too immature to pick, and which are just right, is second nature to seasoned pickers, but for new recruits, it takes a significant learning curve. Mistakes were frequent: flowers were picked too early, or ripe ones were left behind. On top of that, the speed at which harvesting was happening was alarmingly slow.

It quickly became clear that we needed to shift our strategy. We focused our remaining skilled workforce on harvesting and processing to fill existing orders. Meanwhile, the new hires were reassigned to planting tasks. In June and July, we planted the tulip bulbs that had recently arrived from New Zealand, preparing for the Fall and Christmas flower seasons.

With so many new faces, there was a real concern that the company culture, so deeply ingrained in the Sun Valley psyche, could evaporate. On June 16, just one week after that dreadful day, we held a meeting with the entire team. After a round of introductions, I gave a short pep talk. But rather than ending the meeting with a quote, as was our tradition, we opened with a few stirring words from British Prime Minister Winston Churchill, who guided his country through the darkest days of World War II:

> "If you're going through hell, keep going.
>
> Never, never, never give up.
>
> Kites rise highest against the wind, not with it."
>
> Folks, we went through our hell last week. But we kept going, and no, we are not giving up. In fact, just like a kite, we're using this headwind as an opportunity to lift our company higher.

I called this meeting today for two important reasons. First, to introduce the over 100 newcomers who have joined our team in just the last week. And second, to recognize the outstanding performance of the Sun Valley team during one of the most challenging times in our history.

The ICE letter had a twofold effect on this company.

On one hand, it dropped the proverbial neutron bomb, suddenly disallowing 283 of our team members from continuing to work at a company that had been such a meaningful part of their lives.

But on the other hand, something remarkable happened. That same letter had the amazing effect of fusing together those who remained. It gave us a dose of superglue that bonded us in a way we'd never experienced before.

Sun Valley has always been known for its exceptional teamwork. But what we saw this past week was unprecedented. It was heartwarming and inspiring.

As a token of appreciation for your extraordinary efforts, each of you will receive a lunch voucher from your team leader today. It's a small gesture for a big contribution.

Over the last 30 years, we've built a legacy of taking on the hard stuff, troubled companies, run-down farms, abandoned lumber mills, and people who were down and out, and turning those challenges into success stories. We've created opportunity where others saw ruin. We've made a good living for many who came along on this journey.

And let me be clear: we're not stopping now.

Yes, on the surface, this situation may seem insurmountable. But together, we will turn this into something beautiful, something powerful. A defining moment that we'll look back on as a true turning point in our history.

We will rise from the ashes of last week's devastation, with renewed vigor, stronger than ever, and more united than we've ever been.

Let's fly this kite together.

Thank you

CHAPTER 13

WITCH HUNT

God allows us to experience the low points of life in order to teach us lessons we could not learn in any other way. The way we learn those lessons is not to deny the feelings but to find the meanings underlying them.

STANLEY LINQUIST

The summer of 2008 was challenging but still manageable. Our new team members were gradually adapting, and operations stabilized. However, beyond the day-to-day hurdles, a far more serious concern loomed over us: our case had been brought to the U.S. Department of Justice. We were under investigation for potential federal crimes.

ICE agents began visiting both current and former Sun Valley team members at their homes. Some of these visits were part of active investigations into the inner workings of our company, while others involved agents serving subpoenas for individuals to testify before a Federal Grand Jury in San Francisco. Those summoned included our HR director, a former sales and marketing director, members of the HR department, and our CFO. Even individuals no longer affiliated with the company were approached. A former team member living in Portland, Oregon, and my retired administrative assistant were both visited by federal agents.

A troubling moment came when ICE agents arrived at the home of our personnel manager, Mary. She had started her journey at Sun Valley in 1979 as a daffodil picker and had steadily worked her way up through the ranks. By 2008, she was our personnel manager, a respected, long-standing member of the team. That June, she was served with a Federal Grand Jury subpoena. After a grueling legal process that stretched over two-and-one-half years, Mary was ultimately charged with a misdemeanor for knowingly falsifying a single document, specifically, the I-9 form of one team member.

The impact on our team during this time cannot be overstated. Take Fernando, for instance. He had joined Sun Valley in the early 1990s, starting out picking flowers and washing buckets. Over the years, through hard work and dedication, he steadily climbed the ranks. By 2008, he was working in our HR department.

Over Memorial Day weekend that year, Fernando took his family on a short getaway to the caves near Grand Junction, Oregon. The following week, while returning to his car in the parking lot of a grocery store, he was detained by ICE agents, in full view of coworkers who happened to be nearby. The agents brought him in for interrogation and laid out photographs of him and his family at the caves, making it clear they had been monitoring him for weeks.

At the same time, rumors were swirling that ICE was approaching individuals within the company, pressuring them to act as informants. In exchange, they were promised temporary work permits or relief from deportation. Those who refused were threatened with removal from the country. Fernando was one of those who refused to cooperate. As a result, he was arrested and held in a jail in Oakland for four months in an attempt to pressure him into providing information.

He was finally released in February 2009, thanks to protections afforded by his marriage to a U.S. citizen.

But his ordeal didn't end there. He was placed under strict surveillance, required to wear an ankle monitor for the next twelve months. ICE agents routinely parked near his home at night, a quiet but unnerving reminder that they were still watching. We later heard firsthand accounts from team members who had been interrogated by agents standing nose-to-nose with them, screaming: *"You work for us. If you don't, we will ruin you for the rest of your life."* A team member revealed he had been wired with listening devices, his everyday conversations inside the company recorded without our knowledge.

In an effort to ensure full compliance going forward, Sun Valley voluntarily elected to adopt E-Verify using the government's database to confirm that all future hires were legally authorized to work in the United States. At the time, in 2008, fewer than 1% of non-government contracting companies in the country were using E-Verify. What we didn't fully recognize then was how severely this decision would limit our ability to hire the number of workers needed to sustain our operations.

In late August, we received yet another letter from ICE. This time, it stated that 40 team members hired between November 2007 (after the four boxes of I-9s were sent) and June 2008 were deemed ineligible to work in the U.S. On Tuesday, September 2, 2008, we informed this group that they could no longer work for Sun Valley. It was a devastating blow. Losing them further depleted the workforce needed to harvest flowers, pack orders, and plant the next cycle of bulbs.

· · ·

The following morning, Wednesday, September 3, we believed the worst was behind us. I had a teeth cleaning appointment that morning , and while driving to the dentist, I passed Tony's, the local hamburger joint, at 8:00 a.m. I noticed an unusual number of people and vehicles crowded in the parking lot. Some individuals were wearing T-shirts with *ICE* printed boldly across the back.

My first thought was: *This can't possibly be about us. We're done with this. We just let go of the last 40 people yesterday. This must be about another business in the area.*

I merged onto the freeway, continuing on to my dentist appointment. Not even 25 minutes later, while I was in the middle of having my teeth cleaned, Scott Kornberg, our production manager at the time, walked into the dental office. His face was pale, nearly white.

"Lane," he said urgently, "we're having an ICE raid. The farm is surrounded."

I jumped out of the dental chair and rushed out the door with the teeth cleaning bib still dangling from my neck. By the time I reached the farm, the front gate was closed and guarded by ICE agents. After identifying myself, they let me in, and what I saw was shocking. This wasn't a small-scale action. There were agents swarming the premises, 130 in total, who had arrived in 50 vehicles. They had cordoned off the entire facility. A helicopter hovered overhead, and even an airplane circled above, as if a major military operation was underway.

This was not just enforcement; it was a full-scale incursion. The agents had come in with intensity and force, searching for 52 individuals who had not been listed in either of the two previous letters we had received from ICE.

I asked the supervising agent what this was all about, why couldn't this have been handled by a letter, as before, so we could manage the process with dignity and order. He responded that this was a different matter. According to him, the individuals in question had allegedly used Oregon or Washington driver's licenses and falsely claimed to be U.S. citizens or lawful permanent residents, which constituted a federal offense.

When I pressed him on the scale and public nature of the raid, and the lasting spectacle it would create in our local community, he brushed it off, calling it a "soft" and "low impact" operation.

If this was the government's definition of a *"soft" and "low impact" operation*, it raised serious and troubling questions in my mind.

We later learned that 18 of our team members had been detained, each interviewed for approximately 25 minutes before being released. These interviews took place at the local Coast Guard station and, rather than focusing on immigration status or individual conduct, they centered on digging up "dirt" about the company. ICE officials offered these former employees the promise of work permits if they were willing to testify or provide statements against Sun Valley.

What was particularly disturbing was hearing reports that, during and after the raid, certain ICE officials openly stated that their goal was to "bring the company down" and to "shut it down" by the end of the year. These were not just enforcement actions, they felt like an orchestrated attempt to destroy a business that had, up to that point, fully cooperated with every ICE directive and had made a good-faith effort to comply with the law, including our voluntary adoption of E-Verify.

After the ordeal, one question kept echoing in my mind: Why deploy such an enormous, taxpayer-funded operation with 130 agents, 50 vehicles, aerial surveillance, just to interview 18 people?

This ambush-style approach was not only unnecessary; it felt like a betrayal. We had worked in good faith with ICE throughout the process, making painful decisions to comply with each directive we received, and yet we were met with force and suspicion instead of trust and professionalism.

The trauma of that day will never be forgotten by those who were there. The fear, the tears, the handcuffs, it left a mark on everyone. It felt deeply unjust. I couldn't help but reflect on the values this country was founded on. During this painful chapter, profound words from Thomas Jefferson kept ringing in my head: *"When the people fear their government, there is tyranny; when the government fears the people, there is liberty."*

Across the country, an estimated 200,000 companies provide work to approximately 12 million hard-working individuals who present identification documents that, in many cases, could be deemed "suspect" or incorrect. Much of the food we eat is grown and harvested by these very people. And yet, rather than addressing the broader systemic issues, the modus operandi of ICE at the time seemed to focus on targeting certain companies, often industry leaders, especially those located in remote or isolated communities.

Interestingly, our Oxnard farm, located in the heart of a large farming region, was never targeted. It was hard to reconcile the fact that our government seemed to single out a few sheep outside the flock and attack them with such intensity. Many former team members remained in the area, finding jobs in local restaurants, hospitals, hotels, and other businesses

At Sun Valley, we had always strived to be a positive force in our community. We created jobs that had a ripple effect throughout the local economy. We took pride in offering a pleasant, respectful workplace and meaningful benefits. Prior to the events of 2008, those benefits included 100% employer-paid health insurance premiums (including dental and vision), a 401(k) plan with a 50% company match, paid vacation, and much more.

By September 2008, we had lost 370 team members, people who had formed the very heart and soul of our operation. While we deeply appreciated the efforts of the new team members who stepped in, the hard reality was that productivity dropped to just 50% of our normal levels. In a business such as ours, people are the equivalent of oxygen. ICE's step-by-step actions had deprived us of that oxygen. And just as we were gasping for air, ICE appeared poised to strike us again and again. It was a dark chapter in our company's history. I was deeply disillusioned and frustrated, not just by the enforcement tactics, but by the inaction of our elected officials. Despite repeated outreach, there was no progress on comprehensive immigration reform.

After the first blow in June, when we lost 283 people, we managed to partially rebuild our labor force with the help of high school and college students. Thankfully, the summer months tend to be slower in terms of labor demands, so we were able to scrape by. But things took a turn for the worse in September. First, we lost 40 more workers. Then, a day later, another 50 were gone. At that point, the situation had become truly precarious.

September is typically a turning point in the flower business. Demand begins to rise, and harvest volumes increase significantly. At the same time, we enter the critical planting season; larger volumes of tulips, iris, and lilies had to go into the ground to ensure a successful holiday and spring season. That's when the wheels started to come off.

With our workforce dramatically reduced, those left behind were working inordinately long days just to get orders out the door. I remember one Saturday night in particular, standing at the bunching line, helping on the de-bulber until 8:00 p.m. We were exhausted but determined. In the back of my mind, I was already thinking about the next morning, getting up early to take my son Tony and drive for five hours to San Francisco to catch the 49ers game. Somehow, we got the flowers out, but it took everything we had.

Someone later described that time as the team being in a "perpetual holiday mode." And they were right. It's one thing to go all-out for a few weeks leading up to Valentine's Day or Mother's Day, but this had gone on for six relentless months. By the end of 2008, the team was running on fumes, physically and mentally fatigued.

Despite our best efforts, there was one area where we simply couldn't keep up: that was planting the bulbs. We fell behind on our schedules, which in turn threw off the timing for future harvests and holidays. It set off a domino effect that disrupted our production for the next 18 months. Customer confidence wavered, and the long-term consequences were significant.

On February 2, 2012, nearly four years after it all began, we received a letter from ICE that essentially marked the end of their investigation. It was titled simply "Warning Notice." It read: *"The U.S. Government encourages voluntary compliance with the law. As a matter of discretion, we have chosen to issue only this WARNING NOTICE in lieu of imposing any sanctions at this time."*

In other words, ICE was done. But we were left to pick up the pieces. The final toll of this nightmare exceeded well over $15 million and permanently altered the course of our company. One person described it as being stabbed with a dagger in 2008, and then slowly bleeding out for years. It's an image that has stayed with me ever since.

Looking back, that chapter nearly broke us. We were gutted, financially, operationally, and emotionally. But in the middle of that hardship, something deeper began to take shape. The people who stayed, who showed up day after day despite the odds, became more than coworkers, they became a band of brothers and sisters, a core of resilience and quiet strength.

We learned that survival isn't just about getting the job done. It's about holding on to your values when everything around you is being tested. Through it all, the pursuit of purpose remained. It became more than just a phrase, because it was our anchor. Even as we lost ground, we gained something harder to define. The belief that what we were doing, growing flowers, creating jobs, contributing to our community, still mattered.

The storm had stripped us down, but it also revealed who we really were. And that, more than anything, gave us the foundation to keep moving forward.

CHAPTER 14

PICKING UP THE PIECES

*When written in Chinese the word "Crisis" is
composed of two characters: One represents danger
and the other represents opportunity.*

JOHN F. KENNEDY

With the resilience of our team and an unyielding fighting spirit, we pressed forward, despite the staggering odds. In the years that followed, we limped along, always on the lookout for ways to pick up the pieces and rebuild. One casualty of the immigration ordeal was Bart van Haaster, our talented tulip grower in Arcata. His work papers had just expired as we were in the process of extending them in 2008. With no other legal option, he was forced to leave the country.

Fortunately, Haakman New Zealand, one of our tulip bulb suppliers, had an opportunity for Bart, and he relocated there. Two years later, while I was visiting Europe with my daughter Sarah to visit the D-Day landing sites in Normandy, I had a chance to reconnect with Bart and his wife Paula, who were also in Holland on vacation. Bart shared that he had been offered a job in Canada, and it made me think, maybe we should look there ourselves.

At that time, we were shipping a decent volume of tulips to the East Coast of the U.S. Eastern Canada was much closer to our East Coast customers. Despite everything we endured during the immigration crisis, one bright spot that shone through was the growth of our tulip program. From 2000 to 2010, tulips became the primary driver of revenue growth and profitability for Sun Valley.

Demand was strong, and our market share kept increasing. The quality of offshore tulips flown in from Europe was regularly jeopardized due to air transport, while we offered a fresher, stronger product, grown domestically.

For more than 15 years, we steadily converted customers who had once sourced their cut tulips from Holland. But by 2005, we began to see a new shift. Local tulip growers were emerging on the East Coast, in Virginia, Pennsylvania, New Jersey, and Ontario, Canada. Though our tulip sales continued to grow, we did notice a softening of demand from certain customers in the East and Midwest as they began sourcing more locally.

Our vision was clear. We needed to grow tulips closer to our East Coast market. In the summer of 2010, an opportunity presented itself in St. Catherines Ontario, Canada, in a region already home to five other tulip growers. Bart and I went on an expedition to explore the area and found a 150,000-square-foot greenhouse on 17 acres. The greenhouse was in decent condition despite having sat idle for over a year. The property was strategically located, just 20 minutes from the U.S. border, 450 miles from New York City, and 250 miles from Chicago.

For East Coast standards, the Niagara region offered a relatively moderate climate, ideal for tulip production. We purchased the property from the bank at a steep discount. They were eager to offload it before another harsh Canadian winter, one that could destroy the heating system if left unmaintained. It was a win for both sides. Bart rejoined the team, and together we laid out a plan to grow seven million tulips during our first winter season, from January through Mother's Day.

It's important to emphasize that this move wasn't made from a position of prosperity or abundance. It was a strategic decision born out of necessity. We knew that to remain viable as a national tulip supplier we had to secure and grow our business east of the Mississippi. It was a bold move, uncharted territory, but deep down, I believed it was the right step toward restoring the company's long-term health.

We signed on the dotted line in October 2010 and started planting tulips by November. The cooler space at the St. Catherines farm was limited, so we located a secondary cooling facility 25 minutes away in Niagara-on-the-Lake. The building, used by a fruit cooperative, sat idle from October to May, perfectly aligning with our production window. In our first season, we filled about 70% of the space. We harvested the first tulip stems in January 2011.

That's when we hit an unexpected roadblock: resistance from our own customers. We hadn't realized that, at that time, Canadian-grown tulips apparently did not have a great reputation in the U.S. market. Despite our efforts to convince them otherwise, buyers were hesitant.

Let me illustrate the uphill battle we faced with a real example. One of our long- time tulip customers in Minneapolis had been loyal to Sun Valley for years. When we told her we now had tulips available from Niagara, closer to her location and at a more competitive landed cost, she was enthusiastic. "That's great news," she said. But when the purchase order came through, it called for 200 boxes from Sun Valley Arcata and just 20 from Sun Valley Niagara. Confused, we followed up and were told there was no mistake.

She explained that after she'd spoken to her boss, she expressed serious reservations about Canadian-grown tulips, citing poor experiences in the past. That caught us off guard. Despite all our planning and research, this had never surfaced.

Still, we pressed forward. We shipped Niagara-grown tulips to both existing and new customers across the U.S. and Canada, confident in the product's quality and our mission. One question we often got was: *Isn't it more expensive to grow tulips in the cold Canadian climate versus temperate California?* It's a fair assumption, but after several months of operation, we compared gas usage per square foot between the two locations, and found they were nearly identical.

The explanation is surprisingly simple. In Canada, when temperatures drop, the greenhouse windows remain tightly shut. In Arcata, though the outside temperatures are milder, the persistent fog and rain create high humidity. To keep greenhouse humidity below target, the heating pipes must run hot while the windows are slightly cracked to lower the humidity, this is an energy-intensive process.

We also discovered that identical tulip varieties behaved differently in the Canadian winter. Due to colder outdoor conditions, the tulips were shorter, and the buds stayed deeper within the foliage. These nuances were subtle but important, and they helped us better understand how to optimize quality from each region.

Our second season in Canada went much more smoothly. Bart and the team found their rhythm, and we earned the trust of the very customers who

The greenhouse in Niagara

had initially been wary of Canadian-grown tulips. They now saw firsthand that the product coming from Niagara was on par with what we produced in Arcata. We had made some adjustments too, phasing out varieties that tended to be shorter during the coldest months.

We also gained a major new local customer, an upscale Canadian supermarket chain that valued quality and was willing to pay a premium for it. But the real breakthrough came when Walmart awarded Sun Valley the tulip business for all of their divisions across the United States. That decision gave the Niagara location a major boost. We pulled out a map of the U.S. with all of Walmart's distribution center locations and carved up the logistics. Niagara would handle the East Coast DCs, while Arcata would serve the West and Texas. This setup ran smoothly for several years and instantly made Sun Valley Niagara profitable.

Then, in the spring of 2017, Walmart corporate introduced a new "American Made" initiative. Each department was now required to source a percentage of its products domestically. For the floral division, this posed a real dilemma, because the bulk of their flowers came from South America and there was little they could do to meet the new mandate.

The Canadian-grown tulip program became an easy target. For the upcoming season, our Niagara shipments to Walmart were halted. Arcata's volume remained the same, but the Canadian supply was cut off. Ironically, Walmart began sourcing tulips from an East Coast grower who, while marketing themselves as a local grower, actually imported a significant portion of their product directly from Holland. It was a frustrating and, frankly, disheartening development, especially given the effort we had made to build a high-quality, reliable tulip program.

The impact on Niagara was immediate. The Walmart volume had represented a sizable portion of what we produced at the St. Catherines farm. Replacing that business wasn't easy. We were forced to scale back the Canadian operation by more than half, which hit our margins hard.

I had heard the stories and read the case studies about companies that built too much reliance on big retailers such as Walmart. In our case, it didn't cripple the entire business, since Walmart never made up more than 14% of Sun Valley's total sales. However, for the Canadian division, we became another statistic, just as Charles Fishman had described in his book *The Walmart Effect*.

. . .

I typically would visit the farm in Niagara once a month. My routine was well worn. I'd leave Arcata on a Monday evening flight to San Francisco, then catch the red eye to Toronto at 10:00 p.m., landing around 6:00 a.m. From there, I'd grab a rental car and make a stop at the flower auction in Mississauga, just outside Toronto. It was a great opportunity to inspect our tulips before they went to the clock and to compare them side-by-side with those from other regional growers. (It took us several years to finally be accepted as guest members at the auction.)

After the auction, I'd drive an hour to our farm in St. Catherines, usually stopping at my regular Tim Hortons along the way. By 9:30 a.m., I'd arrive at the farm, ready to walk the greenhouse, review the crops, and spend time with Bart and the team. At 12:30, we'd hold our farm meeting with the full crew (more on that in the Sun Valley Culture chapter).

In the afternoon, we'd head to the cooler facility in Niagara-on-the-Lake to check on the tulips in storage. By 3:30 p.m., I was back on the road, navigating Toronto's busy freeways to the airport. I'd catch an early evening flight to Los Angeles, arriving around 9:30 p.m., and would stay at a hotel near the airport.

By 4:00 a.m. the next morning I was up again and headed to the flower market in downtown LA, arriving by 5:00 a.m. I loved walking around the market, checking our flowers, seeing what the competition was up to, and having quick, meaningful conversations with customers. It was a direct line to real-time feedback from the field, and I found those visits invaluable.

By 6:00 a.m., I'd be back in the car to beat the worst of LA's traffic, grab breakfast at McDonald's, and head to our Oxnard farm. I'd arrive just in time for the 7:30 a.m. Zoom call with the teams in Arcata, Oxnard, and Canada. We'd review inventory, production, and sales issues, then begin walking the four Oxnard farm locations with our growers, often joined by a sales team member.

After a quick lunch, usually a Jersey Mike's sandwich in the conference room, we'd finish up the afternoon farm walk by 3:30. From there, I'd drive to the Santa Barbara airport to catch a flight to San Francisco, wait out a layover, and take the final leg home to Arcata. I'd usually walk through our front door just before midnight.

That 48-hour Arcata–Niagara–Oxnard–Arcata roundtrip became a monthly ritual for many years. Occasionally, someone would join me, and after a whirlwind tour like that, they'd joke about making T-shirts that said: *"I survived the Canada trip with Lane."* But more often than not, I made the journey alone.

What kept me going, month after month, was the pursuit of purpose. Staying connected to each farm, each team, and each customer was how I stayed grounded in the mission. It reminded me that leadership isn't found behind a desk, it's found in walking the farm, listening to the people, and showing up, again and again, with conviction.

CHAPTER 15

HOW THE SEEDS WERE PLANTED

May the road rise up to meet you.
May the wind always be at your back.
May the sunshine warm upon your face,
and rains fall soft upon your fields.
And until we meet again,
May God hold you in the palm of His hand.

IRISH BLESSING

Something very interesting began to unfold during my trips to Canada and back, something that would quietly pave the way for my faith-based journey.

After landing in Toronto around 6:00 a.m., sleep-deprived from the red-eye flight, I would struggle to stay alert behind the wheel on my hour-long drive. I flipped through local Toronto radio stations, trying to listen to music, talk shows, anything to help me focus. Nothing worked, until one morning I landed on a station where someone named John MacArthur was giving a sermon. His message was clear, thoughtful, and inspiring. I was immediately drawn in. When MacArthur finished, the next program would begin, this time with Chuck Swindoll, delivering an equally powerful talk. His way of explaining Scripture made the Bible come alive, something I hadn't experienced before. I had attended church for years, but I had read the Bible only sparingly. These broadcasts changed that. They moved me in a way I hadn't expected. From that moment on, whenever I stepped into a rental car in Toronto, the dial automatically went to 99.1 FM.

Later, on a flight from Toronto to Los Angeles, I scrolled through the in-flight entertainment and came across a documentary on the *Dead Sea Scrolls*. I was fascinated. Fifteen-thousand fragments of ancient Scripture, dating back to between the 3rd century BC and 1st century AD, had been discovered between 1946 and 1956. The richness of that discovery, the depth of its historical and spiritual meaning, captivated me.

The seeds of deeper inquiry were planted. Soon, I was searching for more. In LA, after visiting the flower market, I'd get back into the rental car and tune in to a station called KKLA. I timed it so I'd be on the road by 6:00 a.m., partly to beat the traffic, but also because that's when J. Vernon McGee came on with his program, *"Thru the Bible."* With his warm Texan drawl, McGee would walk through a few verses at a time, offering illustrations, insights, and reflections that brought the Scriptures to life.

Those drives, whether to Niagara or Oxnard, became more than just part of a business routine. They became sacred space. Somehow, in all the traffic and turbulence of that chapter of my life, I found stillness, clarity, and an unexpected connection to something far greater than myself. That journey of discovery continued, eventually leading me to the pulpit years later when I was invited to become a lay preacher. (More about that in Chapter titled *The Purpose Journey.*)

CHAPTER 16

THE SUN VALLEY CULTURE

And as we let our own light shine, we unconsciously give other
people permission to do the same. As we are liberated from
our own fear, our presence automatically liberates others.

NELSON MANDELA

W hen I look back, I feel a deep sense of pride in the great team we assembled and the company culture that came to define Sun Valley at its core. Shortly after arriving in Arcata, I developed a hunger for knowledge and began reading business books, looking for information and guidance on how to lead a growing company.

The first business book I read in the 1980s was a gift from my aunt; titled *The Art of Japanese Management* by Pascal and Athos. It was a fascinating book that offered an analytical comparison between management systems in the United States and Japan. Panasonic, led by Matsushita, was presented as an example of Japanese management excellence, while the U.S. was represented by ITT under the leadership of Harold Geneen.

That book became the launching pad for a lifelong search for learning. From there, the list of books I read grew quickly, including titles such as *In Search of*

Excellence by Tom Peters and Robert Waterman, Lee Iaccoca's autobiography, and *The Deming Way* by Mary Walton. I was eager to put some of the ideas I was learning into practice. By the late 1980s, after stepping into the general manager role, we introduced the concept of Quality Circles at Sun Valley.

A Quality Circle is made up of a group of workers who do the same or similar work and who meet regularly to identify, analyze, and solve work-related problems. These groups typically consist of a minimum of three and a maximum of twelve members and are usually led by a supervisor or manager, with solutions presented to management.

The idea of Quality Circles was originally described by W. Edwards Deming in the 1950s, with Toyota often cited as a leading example of the practice. At Sun Valley, we used Quality Circles for many years. They not only helped solve problems on the farm but also gave team members a sense of ownership and pride in the continuous improvement of the company.

The practice of team members contributing to solutions became an integral part of the Sun Valley culture. During our monthly farm meetings we made it a point to recognize team members who had offered valuable suggestions by presenting them with Innovator Awards. The Kaizen-style, continuous improvement culture took deep root at Sun Valley and remained omnipresent throughout all those years.

· · ·

The first time I came across the concept of "managing by walking around" was in Tom Peters' book, *In Search of Excellence*. But there were many other inspiring books along the way, such as the autobiography of Sam Walton, *The J. Willard Marriott Story* about the rise of the Marriott empire, and *Sierra Pacific: A Family History* by J. "Bud" Tomascheski, which recorded Red Emmerson's journey to becoming the largest private landowner in America.

What all these stories had in common was the way their leaders managed—by walking through their facilities daily, staying close to the action, and keeping their ear to the ground.

I adopted this concept early on and made it a personal practice to walk the farm every day. Beyond inspecting the crops, it was the perfect opportunity to stay in touch with what was happening across the different teams. I made it a point to learn as many team members' names as I could, though that got a little more challenging as the company grew.

As Sun Valley expanded, the daily farm walks in Arcata became a set routine. By the late 1980s and into the 1990s, we made a habit of walking the greenhouse and hoophouses with the agronomists every Monday, Wednesday, and Friday, rain or shine. The Tulip Walks happened any day of the week. Even on Sundays before heading to church, I would stop at the farm first and make the loop through the greenhouses to check on the tulips. Saturday afternoons, I often took the kids along with me, driving out to the Del Norte farm, and on Sunday afternoons, we would make the trip to Willow Creek. It's no exaggeration to say that managing by walking around was truly engrained in the Sun Valley culture.

During the first few months after we acquired the Oxnard location, I would take a commercial flight every three weeks to check on the farm there. But it didn't take long for me to realize that this was a little crazy. I was walking the farm in Arcata three times a week, visiting Del Norte and Willow Creek once a week, yet I was visiting Oxnard only once every three weeks, despite its significant production volume and many complexities, including some HR challenges.

I brought this up with someone in my Rotary Club, who happened to own a small Seneca V twin-prop airplane. I asked him what it would take to fly a team of us down to Oxnard every Thursday. That conversation kicked off a new tradition.

Each Thursday, we would leave Arcata at six in the morning, fly down to Oxnard, walk the farms, meet with the local team, and fly back home, usually arriving around 8:00 p.m. Some of those trips were quite memorable. The little Seneca wasn't pressurized, so especially during the winter months, we often found ourselves flying right through the heart of storms rather than cruising above them.

One unforgettable trip to Oxnard gave me the scare of my life. On our way to Oxnard, the airplane engine started sputtering badly when the pilot took the plane above 8,000 feet. He quickly dropped us down to about 7,000 feet and kept it there for the rest of the flight. After we finished walking the farm that afternoon, I asked him if he had the engine issue checked out at the maintenance shop at the Camarillo airport. He shrugged and said, "No, I'll have it looked at when we get back to Arcata."

On the way home, we had to make a quick stop in Watsonville to check something out. By the time we returned to the plane, the folks at the Watsonville airport were buzzing about a huge, violent storm rolling in off the Pacific. Unsuspecting, we climbed into the plane and took off, heading west over the ocean. To avoid the heavy air traffic around San Francisco, the pilot took us far out over the water.

By now it was dark, and way off in the distance, we could just make out the faint glow of San Francisco's city lights. Then the weather hit. Suddenly, the little Seneca was getting kicked all over the sky. It started hailing so hard it felt like the windows could shatter at any moment. Meanwhile, we were getting tossed in every direction. I couldn't help but think about those engines that had been sputtering earlier in the day. Were they going to keep going in these brutal conditions?

Those engines were working as hard as they could, and the thought of them giving out over the open ocean was terrifying. Traveling with me that day was our HR director, who normally loved to talk. But as the violent winds and hail battered the plane, the cabin went completely silent. We both just sat there, hanging on for dear life.

I remember thinking, as far west as we were over the ocean, if we went down, they might never find us. It was one of the few times in my life that I was truly scared.

More than two hours later, we finally touched down safely at the airport near Arcata. After that trip, we decided it was time to find a plane that was a bit more reliable—and pressurized—so we could fly above most of the storms. We ended up connecting with another pilot who flew a Cessna 414. We used that particular plane almost every Thursday for the next two decades.

. . .

One of the core values of the company was team spirit, and we got involved in many events outside our day-to-day work that helped strengthen the camaraderie among the team. We organized a group of volunteers that regularly picked up trash along the freeway. We had a company baseball team, and some years, multiple teams, competing against other local groups. For years, team members also put together a bowling team, and there was even a Sun Valley crew that competed in the local sand sculpture competition.

Sun Valley participated in the Rhododendron Parade in Eureka, the Pony Express Parade in McKinleyville, and the Christmas Truckers Parade in Eureka. We even built a kinetic sculpture and entered the Annual Kinetic Sculpture

Kinetic Sculpture race finish in Ferndale, Calif.

Race. Our mechanic and I spent three days over Memorial Day weekend pedaling and pushing our creation across sand dunes, through Humboldt Bay, and across the Eel River, competing against 60 other sculptures in a wild, uniquely Humboldt event.

The second year we entered, we managed to "ace" the race, meaning we completed all three days without the use of any outside help, and finished in third place. It was a huge source of pride for the team, and just one more way the spirit of Sun Valley carried beyond the farm.

• • •

In 1987, we organized our first Open House. We opened our doors to the local community on a Sunday afternoon, from noon to 4:00 p.m. This tradition continued every year until 2008, and after that, a bit less frequently. The Open Houses were a wonderful way to instill pride in our team members, as they brought their families to see firsthand what mom or dad did each day. It also helped cultivate a lot of goodwill in the community.

Visitors were always blown away by the magnitude of the operation and the intricacies involved in growing flowers. Attendance steadily grew each year, eventually reaching more than 7,000 visitors in just the four hours we were open. One of the big attractions was the general store, where we sold bulbs, Sun Valley merchandise, and fresh flowers. Another highlight was the design competition, with local, regional, and even some national designers competing for the coveted Sun Valley Cup.

Over the years, many people who visited during an Open House ended up joining the Sun Valley team. Putting these events together was not inexpensive, but year after year, the goodwill, community pride, and new relationships made it a very worthwhile investment.

• • •

In 1988, we started a monthly company newsletter filled with stories and pictures of the team, a tradition that lasted for 20 years. The newsletter became an important mode of communication with the team. Particularly as the company was growing, it kept everyone in the loop.

Dottie Haukenberry was my administrative assistant from 1988 until 1998. She was passionate about putting the newsletter together each month. She even dubbed herself "The Roaming Reporter" and had a real knack for being at the right place at the right time. Dottie also provided the administrative support for the Quality Circles.

The concept of the monthly meeting was introduced by Dave Will, who joined us from General Foods. He served as general manager at the Arcata farm in 1986 and 1987. In those early days, the meetings were short, providing quick, concise updates to the team. Everyone would simply stand while Dave spoke for a few minutes, followed by a few words from me in my role as operations manager.

When I stepped into the general manager role in 1988, we made some changes. We built benches so everyone could sit and be a bit more comfortable during the meetings. Early on, we also placed pieces of fruit—apples, oranges, or bananas—on the benches, so everyone had something to munch on while we gathered together and I gave farm updates.

Over time, the meetings grew into more of a gathering, with lunch

Farm meeting in 2004, with Assemblywoman Patty Berg, and Senior Field Representative Connie Stewart in attendance.

served beforehand. Some days it was pizza, other times it was soup and crackers, simple but always appreciated. Early on my updates started with a paper flip chart as I covered production, productivity, safety, and farm spirit. As the years went by, the flip chart gave way to a projector with transparent slides, and later we moved into the digital age with Power-Point presentations.

Before each meeting started, we always had music playing to set the tone. Sometimes, team members would volunteer to share their musical talents during the half hour leading up to the meeting while folks sat together enjoying their soup or pizza. Those moments, filled with laughter, conversation, and the sound of live music, created a real sense of community that carried over into the meeting itself.

Looking back, those meetings weren't just about updates, they were about building a culture, one gathering at a time.

After the Pleasant Valley acquisition in August 2001, followed by Golden Coast Nurseries in October 2001, I admittedly was a bit slow in incorporating the monthly farm meetings at the Oxnard location. My rationale at the time was that we simply didn't have a large enough space to host the meetings. Particularly with two different farms, each with their own separate cultures, the need to unify was larger than I recognized back then.

The first couple of years in Oxnard were not easy, as the teams there had a hard time adjusting to the "Sun Valley" way of tracking data and performance. We did hold some "quasi" farm meetings at the different farm locations in Oxnard, but they never quite yielded the results we were aiming for.

The new building at the Pleasant Valley Road location was completed in the summer of 2003. From that moment on, we began holding farm meetings with all team members from our three Oxnard locations: the Pleasant Valley greenhouse, the Channel Islands Road field operation, and Golden Coast. The impact of these meetings was incredible. Within just a few months, the entire Oxnard team began gelling, and the enthusiasm during the meetings was palpable. There was lots of cheering as we reviewed production numbers.

It became clear that the management approach of sharing numbers and data was making a real difference in morale.

The newsletters soon reflected this momentum as well, featuring an Oxnard section with highlights such as "Team Member of the Period," "Team of the Period," and other newsworthy items that captured the energy and achievements of the team.

From 2006 through 2009 we ran a safety incentive program that really energized the team. Team members who maintained a spotless safety record had their names entered into a raffle, and throughout the year, we gave out all kinds of prizes to recognize their efforts. But the highlight came at the end of the year, when we raffled off a brand-new car at both our Arcata and Oxnard locations. That grand prize created quite a buzz and a lot of excitement across the company.

We had the program fully set up and rolling for several years, but by the end of 2008, things weren't looking good financially. We had taken a hit from the issues surrounding the immigration actions described in previous chapters, and we simply didn't have the funds to go out and buy two brand-new cars. At the same time, I didn't want to cancel the program, because we had made a commitment, and people were looking forward to it.

Back in 2007, I had bought a new Ford F250 and passed my old truck on to one of our managers. Faced with our dilemma in 2008, I asked our CFO to ask the dealer if they would take back my new truck in trade for two cars. Sure enough, it worked. We drove off with two new PT Cruisers, still able to deliver the grand prize in both locations.

I reclaimed my old truck, and it is the truck I am still driving today. It is still going strong.

Prior to 2008, we held a recognition dinner once a year, inviting all team members and their spouses to a nice restaurant in either Arcata or Oxnard to recognize their valued service to the company. Team members who reached tenure milestones, in five-year increments, were honored at these events.

Twice a week, on Tuesdays and Fridays, we also made take-home flowers available to the team. Whenever we had unsold flowers in the coolers, we would set them out for anyone who wanted to take some home. There was almost always something beautiful available. By offering flowers freely it also helped reduce the temptation for folks to take flowers on their own accord.

The Sun Valley Group Supports....

American Legion Post 274
American Lung Association
American Red Cross - Katrina & Tsunami Relief
American Region Baseball
Arcata Chamber of Commerce
Arcata Christian School
Arcata Community Pool
Arcata High Softball
Arcata Main St Oyster Fest
Arcata Rec Division, Youth Basketball
Arcata Rotary Wrestling Tournament
Arcata Youth Baseball
Arcata Youth Football
Arts in the Afternoon Trust Fund
BBBS Bowling pledge
Big Brothers Big Sisters
Blue Lake Fieldbrook Little League
Blue Lake Summer Youth program
Boys & Girls Club
BUDS of the Redwoods
California Farm Bureau (Farm Pac)
CASA
Catholic Charities
Childrens Education Development Society
California Foundation for Ag in the Classroom
City of Eureka, Halloween Carnival
CR Autumn Vintage
CR Foundation
Crescent City Chamber of Commerce
Dairy Princess Committee
Dell'Arte
Discovery Museum
DN Association for Culture Awareness
DN HS Speech Team
DN Rec Dept Youth Basketball
Easter Seals
Eureka Chamber of Commerce Rhodie Festival
Eureka Heritage Society
Eureka High School
Eureka High School/Give Youth a Hand
Eureka HS Safe & Sober Grad
Eureka Rescue Mission
Festival of Trees, Larry McCarty Foundation
Friends of the Dunes, Sand Sculpture
Girls Inc/Northstar Quest
Godwit Days-06
Humboldt County Office of Education Science Fair
Humboldt County Sheriffs Posse
Hospice of Humboldt
Humboldt Arts Council
Humboldt Bay Maritime Museum
Humboldt Classics Snr Softball
Humboldt County Jr Miss Scholarship
Humboldt Crabs Baseball program
Humboldt Harmonaires
Humboldt Hunnies softball
Humboldt Library Foundation
Humboldt Literacy Project
Humboldt Swim Club

Jacoby Creek School
KEET-TV
KHSU
Klamath Bird Observatory
League of Women Voters
Los Bagels Basketball Tournament
Mad River Adult Day Care Center
Mad River Softball Association
Mad River Youth Soccer League
Manila Community Services District
McKinleyville Freestyle Wrestling
McKinleyville High School Booster Club, Safe & Sober
McKinleyville Park & Rec
Muscular Dystrophy
N.C. Soccer League
New World Youth Ballet
North Coast Rape Crisis Team
Northcoast Children's Services
Old Town Rotary, Eureka, Festival on the Bay
Open Door Community Health Center
Orick Chamber-Prince/Princess Contest
PAL Camp
Redbud Theatre, Willow Creek
Redwood Acres Raceway
Redwood Christian School - spaghetti dinner
Redwood Coast Music Festival
Redwood Technology Consortium scholarships
Redwoods Coast Music Fest
Rotary Club of Arcata SunRise, Arcata Fire Dept Fundraiser
Salvation Army
Scotia Bears Cheerleaders
Sequoia Humane Society
Sequoia Park Zoo
Six Rivers Charter High School
Senior Resource Center
So Fork High School Bike Team
Socks for Soldiers
Soroptimist Int'l of Arcata, Inc.
Southern Humboldt Garden Club
Special Olympics No. CA
St Mary's Catholic Church
St. Bernards Catholic School
Sunny Brae Road Runners Basketball Program
This Side of the Rock Fellowship
Timber Heritage Association
Times-Standard, Newspapers in Education
Tri-County Independent Living Center
Tu Casa
Vector Rehab Chocolate Gala
Weitchpec Church
Willow Creek China Flat Museum

We are proud to support a
community that supports us.

Company newsletter 2006, listing community organizations that Sun Valley had supported.

Through the years, Sun Valley took great pride in being known in the local community for its generosity. A company newsletter from 2006 published a list of all the local organizations and events we had supported, a reflection of how deeply rooted giving back was in our company culture.

One of the many community projects Sun Valley supported was the

Sun Valley Greenhouse at Humboldt Botanical Gardens

development of the Humboldt Botanical Garden. In 2005, the Humboldt Botanical Society was in the process of building the garden on 44 acres of land just south of Eureka when they approached us to see if we would be willing to help by building a greenhouse on the site. Construction on the greenhouse began in November of that year, adding an important piece to a project that would serve the community for generations to come.

. . .

Fireworks displays have long been a cherished part of Arcata's Fourth of July tradition. But in 2007, just days before the holiday, the Arcata Chamber of Commerce abruptly announced it would no longer fund the display. The news, reported in the *Arcata Eye* on June 26, sparked an outcry across the community. Upon reading this we immediately reached out and offered to prefund the fireworks that year, inviting others in the community to join us in supporting the effort. We fronted the full cost, and while some individual donations did come in, in the end we covered about 90% of the total expense. Watching those fireworks light up the night sky on July 4, 2007, left us with a lasting sense of purpose and pride in serving the community.

The Sun Valley Christmas parties were something special. We rented the local community centers in Arcata and Oxnard and turned them into festive gathering places for the entire team and their families. Before each party, every team member would submit the ages of their children, and my wife would carefully put together amazing gift baskets tailored to each age group. It was heartwarming to watch all the kids, filled with anticipation, wondering what was inside their baskets, and then to see their faces light up when they received them and started playing with their new toys.

In later years, we moved the Christmas parties into the shipping warehouse, and a new tradition took root, the talent show. Many team members were eager to showcase their musical talents, and every year the managers would perform a song, sometimes dressed up in coveralls and wooden shoes for extra laughs.

We also held annual picnics at both locations, serving a great meal, playing games, and spending the day building connections and camaraderie across the entire Sun Valley team.

Looking back, it was moments like these—the Christmas parties, the picnics, the talent shows—that built more than just a company. They built a family, grounded in a shared sense of purpose, pride, and community that carried us through every season at Sun Valley.

The culture we built kept us strong, but the outside world kept changing too. New challenges started to come our way. In those moments, it was the pursuit of purpose that anchored us, reminding us why we fought so hard to protect what we had built.

CHAPTER 17

THE SPIRIT ILEX JOURNEY

Start by doing what is necessary, then do what is possible,
suddenly before you realize it, you are doing the impossible.

FRANCIS OF ASSISI

S un Valley was always known for its bulb flowers. In the 1960s and 1970s, it was daffodils and iris, By the 1980s, tulips, iris, and lilies had taken center stage.

Since 2000, when the Willow Creek division was conceived, some new key crops came onto the scene, such as Cotinus, Viburnum, and Rosehips, but especially *Ilex verticillata*.

Ilex, the winterberry, is a species of holly. It is prized as an ornamental for use in floral arrangements, particularly for Christmas.

My infatuation with Ilex goes way back to my early years in Holland. Let me illustrate this with an anecdote. Once as I was unloading our van filled with potted plants for the next day's sale at the Aalsmeer auction, I noticed a grower next to me unloading a truck full of Ilex. As he was putting his load onto the auction carts, I struck up a conversation. We got to talking about market pricing, and he told me he was getting one guilder per stem for his Ilex. This was in 1981, when one guilder per stem meant serious money.

A neighbor next to our farm in Beverwijk had a small hobby garden and grew some asparagus for home use. It was November, and some of the asparagus stems had flowered and were now covered in bright red berries. He walked into our greenhouse one day and said, "Look at this, isn't it pretty?"

That got me thinking. My brother and I decided to investigate further. Early on a Saturday morning, we took the van and drove to the province of Limburg in the southeast of Holland, where most of the country's asparagus is grown. After more than two hours on the road, we arrived in Limburg. Many of the fields had already been chopped for the season, but we managed to find some still standing, and sure enough, the stems were loaded with red berries.

We started picking. By midafternoon, our van was filled with what we believed was a newfound treasure. The following Tuesday, we brought our first batch to the Aalsmeer auction. To our delight, we received a decent price, 70 cents per stem. But just two days later, things didn't go so well. The price had dropped to only 23 cents. Apparently, the buyers at the clock had figured out that these weren't Ilex at all, but that they were asparagus stems. That was the end of our pseudo-Ilex venture.

We never considered growing Ilex at our farm in Beverwijk because the soil pH simply wasn't suitable. And after moving to the U.S. and settling in Arcata, Ilex was again not on my radar, for the simple reason that while Arcata's climate is ideal for bulb flowers, it's not favorable for Ilex.

That all changed in 2000. We planted our first 460 Ilex plants at the farm in Willow Creek. They came from a grower in Boskoop, Holland, and were of the *Oosterwijk* variety. What we didn't realize at the time was that propagating Ilex from cuttings is not easy, and some plant suppliers take shortcuts by offering seed-propagated plants instead. As a new and inexperienced customer, we must have been an easy target.

Several years later, when the first stems were ready for harvest, we noticed some inconsistencies in the crop but didn't think much of it at first. What truly caught our attention was one plant, a bit shorter than the rest, but with striking orange berries.

We showed the plant with the orange berries to Peter Kolster—a plant supplier from Boskoop, Holland, as well—during his visit to the Willow Creek farm in the fall of 2003. Peter was intrigued, he took some material back with him, intending to graft it onto Ilex rootstock at his nursery in Holland.

He named the variety Magical Times, and we agreed to split the proceeds from any future plant sales in Holland. But as it turned out, the cuttings Peter took the following summer from the grafted material included some shoots that had developed from the rootstock itself. It took two full growing seasons to realize that these had been mixed in, causing a major setback in production.

Eventually, in 2009, we received 1,500 true Magical Times plants and planted them at our Willow Creek farm. Unfortunately, the variety was not a strong grower. Even in Willow Creek's favorable climate, it remained relatively short. In Holland, with its cooler climate and fewer sun hours, Magical Times didn't perform at all. Despite its striking orange berries, the variety never took off. At the flower auctions, buyers pay for length, and these stems were simply too short.

Meanwhile, back at the ranch in Willow Creek, we were planting new fields of Ilex almost every year with mostly *Oosterwijk* (red) and some *Golden Verboom* (light orange), the standard varieties in Holland. In the early years we harvested from the same fields every year, but we eventually learned a better approach. It was much more beneficial to harvest all the stems from a field in one season, prune plants all back and let them grow vegetatively the following year (one-year wood). In the second year the whole crop is ready for harvest again, yielding better quality and uniformity.

By 2004, we took some berries from that orange-berried plant (Magical Times), that had been mixed in with the initial planting and decided to propagate it from seed. We had two reasons for this. First, at the time, we were still struggling to master propagation from cuttings. The results just weren't very good. Second, we hoped that growing from seed might yield new orange-berried Ilex variations, ideally ones even better than the original *Magical Times*, and certainly more productive than *Golden Verboom*, which tended to produce berries only halfway up the laterals.

One of the ongoing challenges with varieties like *Oosterwijk* and *Golden Verboom* is their vigorous growth. While that might sound like a good thing, it actually works against the goal of producing a compact, densely berried stem. To manage this, Ilex growers in Holland often resort to spraying growth retardants like Alar or use techniques such as root-cutting to stunt the plant and force a tighter berry set.

After collecting berries from the original *Magical Times* plant in 2004, we germinated the seeds in our propagation house the following year. By spring of 2006, we planted 2,000 seedlings, each one a potential new variety, derived from that single, orange-berried plant.

One thing we noticed right away was the diversity among the seedlings, but even more striking was their vigor and vitality. The growth characteristics

The original seedling field in Willow Creek

were noticeably stronger than the other Ilex varieties growing in the neighboring fields.

By the fall of 2007 some of the first seedlings began showing stems with berries, much earlier than we had expected. To my surprise, though, very few of the ones showing color were actually orange. Instead, most displayed shades of light red, what we came to refer to as "Flames."

That year, I selected 86 plants that stood out, either for their color or other desirable plant characteristics. It was an exciting beginning, even though the orange berries we had hoped for were still absent.

I had one big concern: that the tags I used to mark the promising seedlings could get lost, blown away by the wind, or pulled off by animals. (We later discovered that bears actually have a taste for Ilex.) I came up with a system to track everything more reliably. Each row was given a letter designation, and each plant within the row was assigned a number. For example, a seedling labeled D-5 came from row D and was the fifth plant in that row.

Once reaching the end of the alphabet, the next 26 rows were labeled with double letters, and after that, triple-letter combinations. The field ended up consisting of 64 rows, so only the last 12 rows used triple-letter designations.

In 2007, I began recording every seedling that produced berries, using a detailed set of criteria. I noted the number of harvestable stems and measured their length. I rated the berry density on a scale from light to very heavy, while also recording the length of the laterals, short, medium, or long. Another key factor was berry coverage along the lateral, ranging anywhere from 30% to 100%, which soon became one of the most important drivers in the selection process. I also categorized berry size as medium, large, or extralarge, and finally assessed the overall plant habit, paying attention to height, girth, and general visual appeal.

To bring order to this maze of traits, I created a scoring system. I assigned numerical values to each factor: berry density was scored from 6 (medium) to 10 (very heavy), lateral length was measured in inches, berry coverage ranged from 3 (30%) to 10 (100%), and berry size was scored as 6 (medium),

8 (large), or 10 (extra-large). The final criterium, overall height and girth, was rated on a scale from 4 to 10. To reflect its importance, berry coverage on the lateral was given extra weight in the final score, multiplied by a factor of three. This system allowed for objective comparison and helped surface the most promising selections from the field.

This scoring system proved invaluable in identifying the best-performing selections. Each fall in 2007, 2008, and 2009, I walked the field every weekend, clipboard in hand, evaluating and recording noteworthy seedlings. By 2009, the number of promising selections had grown into the hundreds.

That same year, in row GG, plant #11 caught my eye. It had all the characteristics we were looking for with strong vigor, dense berry set, excellent lateral coverage, and, most exciting of all, orange berries. This selection, GG-11, would eventually become known as *Autumn Spirit*. It stood out not only for its vibrant color but also for its earliness, producing colored berries by the last week of August, making it one of the earliest varieties to reach market at the onset of the Ilex season.

In the winter of 2009–2010, we pruned back the entire field to reset the plants and bring them into a rhythm consistent with a commercial

Ilex selection work during the fall

production cycle. That meant that in the fall of 2010 there was nothing to evaluate visually, as all the growth was one-year wood preparing for the following season.

Meanwhile, we had made two attempts at propagation in 2008 and 2009, taking cuttings from our most promising selections. But, admittedly, our results were poor. So, in 2010, we had vegetative growth (one-year wood), which is perfect for propagation. We selected 46 of our top-performing plants, took cuttings from each, and shipped them to Kolster in Holland. The hope was to jump-start our propagation program and accelerate the path to commercial production of these varieties and for Kolster to test these varieties under Dutch growing circumstances.

In August 2010, Jacob Rooijakkers, one of my Dutch partners, passed away. While in Holland to attend his funeral, I also took the opportunity to visit Kolster and check in on the progress of the Ilex cuttings we had sent. That visit turned out to be a turning point in our propagation journey.

Seeing their cuttings operation firsthand and talking through the techniques with Kolster was truly invaluable. I came away with practical insights that transformed our own approach. From 2011 onward, we began propagating Ilex ourselves with much greater success. This allowed us to scale up our program and build a foundation based entirely on our own selections.

By late August 2011, the berries on the seedlings began coloring up again, and the selection process entered a new chapter. Remarkably, several standout varieties emerged that hadn't caught my attention in the previous three years. One in particular, BB-9, stood out in every way. This was a true red variety with prolific stem production, a heavy berry set, and berries on many of the stems that occupied 100% of the lateral. On top of that, the berry size was excellent. In every respect, this plant checked all the boxes.

I felt that the Lord had blessed me with a winner. That selection would eventually be named *Winter Spirit*, a variety that would go on to win awards and become one of the anchors of our Ilex program. More than just a breakthrough variety, *Winter Spirit* represented a moment where years of trial, observation, and faith came together, confirming that there was real purpose behind the process.

Ilex selections 2007 +2008+2009+2011

row#	stems 2007	2008	2009	cuttings 2011	stumps 2011	stems 2011	total 2011	color (8-Nov 2009)	leng obs	berry density	score	later leng with berries	berries% of lateral	score	size of berry	score	heigh strenght	over	take cutti sep	take cutti dec	collec seed	Kol	overa score
Y 22	4		8			25	25	light red	30	H	8	8	60%	6	L	8	6						73
Z 14	3					8	8	light red	28	V	10	6	60%	6	L	8	5						55
AA 5	4	5		yes	16	0	16	light red	33	V	10	3	100%	10	L	8	6		grea	yes	yes	yes	73
AA 26	2					14	14	light red	28	L	6	8	50%	5	M	6	7						56
BB 7	2					12	12	light red	28	H	8	3	100%	10	M	6	4		weak plant				63
BB 9			NEW			23	23	red		H	8	3	100%	10	L	8	10						**82**
BB 10	5					6	6	light red	27	V	10	3	80%	8	L	8	6		not good				57
BB 30	1	2				10	10	red	34	L	6	5	60%	6	M	6	8						53
CC 8	3	7				16	16	oran dark o	31	L	6	5	50%	6	M	6	6		berries drop	yes			54
DD 3	3					2	2	red	28	L	6	6	50%	6	XL	10	3						42
DD 7	3	0				0	0	light red	32	H	8	6	40%	4	L	8	4						38
DD 20		9				20	20	light red	40	H	8	4	70%	7	M	6	6						65
EE 5	4					12	12	light red	28	L	6	8	40%	4	M	6	4						48
EE 21	3					7	7	oran red	32	VH	10	6	50%	6	XL	10	4					yes	52

One of the scoring sheets for each of the seedlings

We began propagating from that single *Winter Spirit* plant, using the techniques I had observed during the visit to Kolster's farm. The following year, we planted our first block of *Winter Spirit* at the Willow Creek farm. As the years went on, older *Oosterwijk* fields, many more than 15 years old, were systematically replaced with *Winter Spirit* and other promising new selections. While Ilex fields can remain productive for decades, the economics made the decision clear. The average yield for an *Oosterwijk* plant was about 12 to 15 stems per production cycle. In contrast, *Winter Spirit* consistently produced between 22 and 28 stems per cycle.

Through a fellow Ilex grower, we also trialed *Winter Red* and *Maryland Beauty*. Both produced impressive, thick stems, but plant yields remained low, just 8 to 12 stems per cycle. It didn't take long before we phased out those varieties as well.

Comparison of Oosterwijk and *Winter Spirit* ™

Oosterwijk   •   *Winter Spirit*

Our pursuit of new variety types had been sparked. In 2009, we collected seed from a number of outstanding seedlings and planted them in Willow Creek in 2011. But two years later, to my great disappointment, very little stood out in this new selection field. It was a humbling reminder of just how blessed we had been with the first field planted in 2006, what we referred to as the *F1 seedlings*. The field that had produced *Winter Spirit* and *Autumn Spirit*.

The 2011 planting, which we came to call the *F2 seedling field*, was largely underwhelming, except for two exceptions. One of those was B-43-4, selected in August 2013. This plant bore a striking pumpkin-orange color, had strong stem production, high berry density, 100% berry occupancy on the laterals, and impressively large berries. Sarah Houle, Business Development Manager at Central Markets in Texas was visiting that year and this selection very much caught her eye. That selection would eventually be patented and introduced under the name *Pumpkin Spirit*, a vibrant addition to our growing Ilex family.

An essential element in Ilex production is pollination, female plants require male plants nearby, and bees to do the work during bloom. The general rule is to plant 10% males among 90% females. But one critical insight we gained through years of hands-on experience was just how important bloom timing is. The original *Oosterwijk* variety, for instance, blooms relatively late in the season, around the third week of June, and Kolster had provided male plants that matched that window. However, we discovered that many of our new selections bloom much earlier. For instance, *B-43-4* (*Pumpkin Spirit*) starts blooming in the second half of May and continues for about 10 days. *BB-9* (*Winter Spirit*) blooms around the first week of June.

This meant we had to find male plants that matched these bloom times exactly. Without synchronized

Pumkin Spirit TM

(B-43-4) USP# PP31,749

bloom windows, even the most promising selection would suffer from poor berry set. Understanding these intricacies became part of our larger pursuit.

To get a better handle on the bloom timing of all these selections, I bought a beekeeper's hat. In the early summer of 2014, I suited up in that hat and full raingear and spent several hours each Saturday afternoon, sometimes in 80-degree heat, for about five weeks, carefully recording the blooming times of each selection. It wasn't glamorous work, but it was essential. During those sessions, I also tagged a number of male plants with strong growing characteristics and recorded their bloom windows. From this effort, I developed a system grouping all selections into six distinct bloom-time categories. That system became a key tool in pairing each female selection with the right male, ensuring strong pollination and consistent berry set.

During the selection period in the F2 field, I came across one plant that began as a yellow and shifted to a more golden tone. Visually, it was promising, but it lacked the essential traits of berry density, lateral coverage, and berry size. Still, I was curious. So, in 2013, we took seed from that plant, along with seed from several orange selections and one red selection and sowed them for the next generation. These *F3 seedlings* were planted in the field in 2015.

Ironically, the golden-seeded plant yielded nothing of significance. The real surprise, however, came from the red-seeded variety. From this plant came a standout seedling, selected on August 26, 2017, named C-11-46-77-23. It displayed vibrant yellow-orange berries that matured into a soft, pale orange gold over the following weeks.

Its performance was exceptional, with dense berry set, short 2-inch laterals with 100% berry coverage, large berry size, and strong overall plant vigor. Altogether, these attributes earned C-11-46-77-23 a place among our very best. Its color was reminiscent of *Golden Verboom*, but it surpassed it in production and berry presentation on the stem.

That selection was eventually patented and introduced to the market as Gold Spirit.

The pipeline of new selections continues with a series of *F4 seedlings* showing some very promising yellow varieties that carry forward the same exceptional characteristics as their ancestors. It's still too early to describe them in detail at the time of this writing, but the early signs are truly exciting.

GOLDEN
VERBOOM

GOLD
SPIRIT™

More than 40 years after picking those asparagus berries from that field in Holland, I feel we have made our mark in the Ilex world. Today, Spirit Ilex varieties are grown by more than 20 growers across the U.S., Holland, Canada, and the U.K. What started with curiosity and a handful of seeds has grown into a purposeful effort to elevate the standard of Ilex, and I'm deeply grateful to have been part of that journey.

CHAPTER 18

A PASSION FOR FLOWER PROMOTION

No matter what people tell you, words
and ideas can change the world.

ROBIN WILLIAMS

S un Valley has always aimed to lead, not just in growing flowers, but also in how we tell our story. From the beginning, we believed that promoting our crops wasn't just about selling flowers but was also about sharing our passion and purpose with the floral community in the U.S. In the 1990s, we ran frequent ads in industry-wide periodicals. One of the most memorable was our "Dream Team" campaign during the 1992 Olympics, featuring our newest Oriental lilies, an ad that reflected both innovation and pride in our work. Over the years, we created a series of posters highlighting our signature lily and iris varieties, culminating in a grand poster in 2007 that showcased every flower we were growing at the time.

Nearly two decades ago our New Zealand Tulip bulb suppliers came knocking, looking for help promoting fall-flowering tulips in the U.S. We embraced the challenge wholeheartedly and coined the phrase *"Spring Quality in the*

Fall," a nod to the fact that these bulbs were six months younger than their Dutch counterparts because the months of September and October were their natural spring. The campaign took off, and within 15 years, we were growing more than 29 million tulips annually from Southern Hemisphere bulbs.

Our website became an essential tool for customers nationwide, offering real-time insight into what was blooming and available throughout the seasons. In 2010, we took our outreach a step further by launching a weekly blog, diving deep into the details of different crops. These posts were purposeful. They educated, inspired, and connected people to the beauty and complexity of what we do. And in a lasting testament to that effort, many of those blog posts still show up today when someone searches for a particular flower crop. It wasn't just about marketing, but also about living out our purpose through every channel available.

On March 8, 2009, Debbie Hartman, who managed our greens department, approached me and said, "Today is Women's Day. Wouldn't it be great if, someday, all women in America received flowers on this day?" I loved the idea. There was something deeply meaningful about honoring women with

Debbie Hartman

flowers, not just on Mother's Day or Valentine's Day, but on a day that recognized all women for their broader contributions to society.

We began researching and discovered that the first Women's Day was celebrated in 1909 in New York City, and was originally called "National Women's Day." By 1910, it had taken off globally. In places such as Russia and much of Eastern Europe, Women's Day became the predominant flower holiday. It struck us as a missed opportunity here in the U.S., not just commercially, but also in purpose.

The following year, on March 8, 2010, I happened to be in Washington, D.C., for the Society of American Florists' Congressional Action Days. We prepared 20 boxes, each filled with 20-stems tulip bouquet. I gathered a group of volunteers, about 25 of us in total, and we handed out the bouquets to women in Georgetown. The response was incredible. Smiles, gratitude, and many pictures. That simple act of giving flowers sparked something real. It became the launch point for a movement to promote Women's Day as a flower-giving holiday in America. In that moment, flowers became more than a product, they became a gesture of purpose.

The team of volunteers ready to take the flowers to Georgetown in 2010

In 2012, I was invited to give a presentation at the Super Floral Show in Miami, Florida. At the time, I was serving as chairman of the California Cut Flower Commission (CCFC), and the show organizers asked me to share my perspective on the state of the domestic flower industry. The presentation was data-heavy, but at its core, it carried a clear message that the American flower industry was in need of revitalization. One of the key opportunities I highlighted was the potential of Women's Day, not only as a new sales opportunity, but also as a cultural movement to increase floral consumption in the U.S.

In the early years, Sun Valley took the lead in promoting Women's Day. We printed special stickers and placed them on all of our flower sleeves, except in supermarkets that specifically requested not to use them. These stickers began appearing on February 15th and continued through early March, helping to build awareness week by week. We also had our box manufacturer create custom Women's Day shipping boxes, which carried our flowers throughout the country in the lead-up to March 8th.

These were intentional marketing efforts to plant the seed of a new tradition. A tradition rooted in respect, appreciation, and the simple but powerful gesture of giving flowers to honor women.

Women's Day printed boxes prior to the holiday

In 2012, Whole Foods ran a Women's Day promotion featuring 20-stem tulip bunches. It turned out to be a tremendous success. The positive response was so strong that Whole Foods continued the promotion for many years afterward.

In 2014, the Society of American Florists honored us with the Floral Marketer of the Year award. The cover of *Floral Management* magazine marked the moment by dubbing me "Mr. Women's Day."

Following is the speech I gave while accepting this prestigious award.

Ladies and Gentlemen, members of the flower industry, good morning.

My name is Lane DeVries, and I am a California flower farmer.

On behalf of the Sun Valley team, it is a great honor to stand here today and for our company to be the recipient of this coveted award.

One of the Sun Valley guiding principles is: Always be humble and gracious.

In light of this we had some trepidation about even submitting the application for this award and rather sidestep the spotlight.

We eventually did submit but not because this is about Sun Valley.

No... highlighting the successes up to now speak more to the potential for our industry than is it about our company.

I believe the American flower industry won today. As we are gathered here together we represent the industry.

A few years ago, I was asked to give a presentation at an industry event in Miami.

The data that I pulled for that presentation actually underscored that the American flower business is ripe for a transformation.

Based on USDA data using a combination of port of entry values for all imports and total domestic farm gate values provided a producer value that increased from 800 million dollars in 1989 to 1.3 billion dollars in 2012, or 64% in 24 years

Meanwhile, GDP growth over this same period increased by 186%.

In other words, as a subset of the national economy the flower industry share actually decreased by 43%.

Looking at the international arena, we see that countries such as Switzerland, Japan, Holland, and the U.K. are in top quartile with flower consumption of $80 to $115 per capita.

The U.S. is in the bottom quartile group with consumption of $20 to $25 per capita; countries such as Greece, Italy, and Slovenia actually exceed flower consumption of the U.S.

Folks, I don't know about you, but these numbers make me edgy. They underscore the need for all of us to have an open mind towards change. As a floral community we need to become less Valentines Day and Mother's Day centric and look for additional opportunities to drive sales.

There are countless dormant holiday possibilities. But Women's Day is the low hanging fruit and the perfect holiday to bolster sales.

First of all, it is an American holiday. It was started in New York City more than one hundred years ago.

In Russia and many European countries Women's Day has become the predominant flower holiday.

Flexibility is ideal, as no particular color or flower type is required.

But the most powerful attribute of this holiday is that 50% of the population is eligible to receive flowers that day.

In closing: Once again we are deeply honored for the recognition.

This day will help lift Women's Day to the next level in America.

I hereby would like to donate back the $5,000 check to the SAF PR fund with an earmark towards Women's Day promotion.

I leave you this morning with a hope, a dream, an innate desire, and an unshakeable conviction that someday our country will be in the top quartile of flower consumption, as the American flower industry COLLECTIVELY embraces this holiday.

Thank you and God bless you.

The standing ovation after that speech seemed to go on forever. But from that day forward, Women's Day was indeed lifted to a new level. Following the SAF recognition, Michael LoBue, then executive director of CalFlowers—with the help of other industry trade groups—offered support to help cover the cost of printing Women's Day posters. These posters were distributed to supermarkets and wholesalers across the country. FTD also stepped in, including a Women's Day poster among the many promotional materials they regularly sent to their network of florists.

Meanwhile, the same stickers we printed for flower sleeves ahead of the holiday became a familiar and beloved sight at industry events. Over the last decade, attendees at virtually every major floral convention have been decorated with one, or often several, Women's Day stickers. It's amazing how much people love stickers.

Since 2018, during the American Tulip Day event in San Francisco, everyone picking tulips also received a Women's Day sticker. And if we ever missed someone, they would come back asking for "their" Women's Day sticker.

All these efforts combined have helped elevate Women's Day into a vibrant floral holiday. Over the past decade, it has become widely embraced by the American floral industry. In 2022, I was deeply honored to receive the Floral Marketer of the Year award from the International Fresh Produce Association (formerly PMA), a humbling recognition given the many outstanding professionals in our industry.

When it comes to social media, I was very much a latecomer; I didn't start my own Instagram account until 2018. But walking around the farms in Arcata, Oxnard, or Willow Creek always presented ample opportunities to take pictures. Winter, in particular, brought a steady stream of tulip varieties, creating a continuous supply of visual content. I started a post called "Tulip of the Week," featuring a bunch of 30 stems displayed on the kitchen counter in our home. With so many varieties available, there was always a new one to showcase each week. Gradually, the Instagram following began to grow.

lanedevries

View insights   Boost post

♡ 37.9K   ◯ 27   ◁ 2,453

Liked by americangrownflowers and others
lanedevries This week, a tulip variety on the kitchen counter called 'Dutch Lane'. A light pink... more
May 9, 2023

By the spring of 2022, the account had about 5,000 followers. Then, in March, I posted a short video of people picking tulips in Union Square during American Tulip Day in San Francisco just days prior to Women's Day. That post went viral, reaching over 600,000 views and doubling the follower count to more than 10,000 in just a few weeks.

Building on the momentum of Women's Day, I see tremendous opportunity to replicate this approach and develop additional floral holidays, especially during the summer months, when our industry needs it most. Promoting flowers and finding new ways to increase floral consumption in the U.S. has always been a passion of mine, and without a doubt, one of the enduring pillars in my pursuit of purpose.

Looking ahead, I believe the future of the industry depends on our ability to inspire, to innovate, and to connect with people in meaningful ways. Flowers have the unique power to brighten lives, mark important moments, and bring beauty into everyday spaces. If we can continue to tell that story, through social media, through community events, and through fresh ideas such as Women's Day, we can ensure that flowers remain an essential part of American culture. It's a challenge worth embracing, and one I remain committed to in the years to come.

CHAPTER 19

HEADWINDS IN CALIFORNIA

When you're playing against a stacked deck, compete even harder.
Show the world how much you'll fight for the winner's circle.

PAT RILEY

W hile we were still picking up the pieces from the 2008 immigration crisis and trying to climb out of the financial hole it left behind, the business climate in California had only grown more difficult. For years, California has consistently ranked among the worst states for doing business, especially for small firms. In 2015, the *Pacific Research Institute's Small Business Regulation Index* placed California dead last. This view was later echoed by the *Small Business and Entrepreneurship Council* in 2019 (49th place), and by the *Cato Institute* in 2021, which ranked California 48th in its study on the best and worst states for entrepreneurs. *Chief Executive* magazine, which surveys over 600 CEOs each year, ranked California fiftieth, dead last, in its 2023 list of best states for business.

The message from business leaders across the country is clear, California is the most challenging state in which to operate a business.

According to the Sacramento-based *Center for Jobs and the Economy*, since 2020, more than 500 companies have either left California entirely or significantly scaled back their in-state operations in favor of expanding elsewhere. The reasons are well known: punishing regulations, high taxes, mounting fees, and an overall cost of doing business that's among the highest in the nation. Many companies have simply "voted with their feet."

Since 2014, the state minimum wage has increased by 83%. On top of that, California has led the way in regulating agricultural overtime. In many other states, and in Canada, there are no overtime rules for agricultural workers.

Since the 1970s California has maintained a bifurcated system. Overtime for field laborers started after 60 hours per week, while overtime for warehouse roles like packing and processing was triggered after 40 hours. But that changed with Assembly Bill 1066 (AB 1066), the *Phase-In Overtime for Agricultural Workers Act of 2016*, signed into law by Governor Jerry Brown on September 12, 2016.

Before 2008, we proudly paid wages above the state minimum. But after the immigration meltdown, and especially in the wake of aggressive wage hikes, our entry-level wage dropped to the legal minimum. While many team members still earned more, the rapid, state-mandated increases compressed the entire wage structure. The elimination of the 60-hour threshold for overtime further increased our labor costs.

It's not just the rules, it's also how they're applied. Take, for example, a week in which a crew works 9.5 hours on Monday, then 8 hours Tuesday and Wednesday, and 7 hours on Thursday and Friday. Their weekly total is just 39.5 hours. But because California mandates overtime calculation on a daily basis, not weekly, we were required to pay 1.5 hours of overtime for Monday's extra time, even though the total hours fall short of a standard 40-hour week.

In parallel, California has enacted a host of wage and hour laws that have opened the floodgates to class-action litigation. Many of my colleagues have faced painful legal battles and ended up settling for significant sums, even in cases involving minor, technical violations. In our situation the judge threw a case against us out of court, but not before we spent more than a million dollars in attorney fees defending our case.

These are just some of the factors that have made it increasingly difficult to do business in California. Layer by layer, the state has placed more and more pressure on our ability to stay competitive, invest in our people and the company as a whole, and keep the ship on course.

CHAPTER 20

PROFLOWERS/FTD

*Success is not final; failure is not fatal: it is the courage
that counts. The price of greatness is responsibility.*

WINSTON CHURCHILL

In the summer of 1998, Proflowers reached out to see if we'd be interested in shipping flowers directly to their customers. This was a new concept for us; we had never shipped directly to consumers before. We agreed to give it a try, and by that fall we were sending out a handful of boxes each day.

Then came Valentine's Day 1999, and what we thought was a big deal. By the time we packed and shipped the last boxes on Friday, February 12th, we were pretty proud of ourselves. In the five days leading up to the holiday, we had packed and shipped 2,636 boxes. Little did we know what was in store for us in the years ahead.

In July 1999, Proflowers CEO Bill Strauss flew to Arcata to meet with me. He shared that based on customer feedback from the previous eight months, Sun Valley ranked as their number one flower vendor in terms of quality scores. Based on that performance, he wanted to have a serious conversation about doing more business together.

The following Valentine's Day, we shipped more than 23,000 boxes to Proflowers customers. For Mother's Day that same year, we shipped more than 41,000. By the end of 2000, Proflowers had become our largest customer, a distinction they would hold for 14 straight years.

As Proflowers grew, we grew with them. In the early years, all shipping happened directly from our farms, first in Arcata, and later in Oxnard as well. I vividly remember one particular Mother's Day in the early 2000s when we were running low on tulips as the holiday approached. We were starting to panic. Proflowers was expecting to ship 45,000 boxes out of Arcata.

What we *did* have plenty of was iris. I called Bill Strauss and asked if they could highlight iris on their website instead of tulips. To my surprise, he said, "Let's try it and see what happens." Their team created a new SKU for a bouquet of 20 iris stems and placed it, front and center, on the site.

In no time, the iris orders started rolling in. By the time the holiday shipping ended, we had moved 20,000 boxes or 400,000 stems of iris in just five days. It was a tremendous help to us and a great example of the agility that defined Proflowers in those early years.

Proflowers boxes ready for shipment

The peak of our direct shipping partnership with Proflowers came in 2005. In the five days leading up to Mother's Day we shipped more than 173,000 boxes from the Arcata and Oxnard farms directly to Proflowers customers. It took an extraordinary effort to make that happen. I remember standing there on the packing line myself, right alongside the sales manager, the administrative team, basically anyone we could pull in to get boxes out the door. It was all-hands-on-deck.

Another vivid memory comes from Mother's Day shipping in 2010. We were running low on iris in Arcata, which we needed to mix with tulips for the tulip/iris bouquet. Things were getting precarious. On my way back from Oxnard on a Thursday afternoon, we loaded the plane full of iris. I remember sitting in my seat with bunches of iris stacked all around me. The moment we landed, a crew was already waiting at the airport to rush the flowers back to the farm, where the night shift would assemble the bouquets for shipping the next morning.

As Proflowers grew, they eventually developed their own network of fulfillment centers across the country. Our role evolved from just packing boxes in Arcata and Oxnard to also shipping bulk flowers to their regional hubs. The logistics became increasingly complex. For major holidays such as Valentine's Day and Mother's Day, we would rent temporary cooler space in places such as Sacramento or Watsonville. Trucks from Arcata and Oxnard would deliver the flowers to these staging locations, where a team of seasoned Sun Valley members would manage consolidation. From there, Proflowers arranged transportation to their fulfillment centers nationwide.

The partnership continued to grow, and by 2014, we hit the peak, with more than 1 million Proflowers bouquets shipped from Arcata and Oxnard for Valentine's Day and Mother's Day combined.

That same year, on December 31, 2014, FTD purchased Provide Commerce, the parent company of Proflowers, for $430 million. The deal created a combined company with more than $1 billion in revenue.

But with the acquisition, things began to change. The company culture that had been carefully cultivated under Bill Strauss's leadership for 16 years started to fade quickly under the new ownership. FTD struggled to integrate the two companies, weighed down by massive overhead in both their Chicago and San Diego offices. The once-relentless focus on quality, a hallmark of Proflowers, began shifting toward a price-driven model, designed to offset the bloated cost structure of the new organization.

Ironically, with the creation of a much larger company, we expected our business with them to grow. Instead, it began to decline. By the end of 2015, Proflowers/FTD was no longer our largest customer. The volumes remained substantial, but the nimbleness and market responsiveness we had come to rely on were replaced by a rigid and often slow-moving corporate structure. Leadership turnover became another concern, as CEO after CEO cycled through the company.

By 2018, we were still shipping around 800,000 bouquets for Valentine's and Mother's Day combined. But in 2019, that number dropped sharply to just over 500,000. The real challenge came from the lack of communication. FTD had indicated that volumes would be similar to the previous year, so we had made preparations accordingly. When the actual orders fell far short, it left us scrambling to find new customers for flowers that FTD had failed to take. It caused serious disruption and frustration for our team.

Then, the final blow came just three weeks after the close of Mother's Day shipping. On Friday, May 31, we learned that FTD had implemented a major reorganization. Many employees had lost their jobs, including the president of the Proflowers division, my main point of contact. I felt the ground shifting beneath us. That weekend, I sat down and wrote a letter to Scott Levin, the CEO of FTD.

Mr. Levin,

By way of introduction, my name is Lane DeVries, CEO of the Sun Valley Group. I am a fourth-generation flower farmer who emigrated from Holland 36 years ago and co-founded Sun Valley in 1991. Today, we employ over 700 team members across four locations in the United States and Canada.

Our company has maintained a longstanding partnership with FTD/Proflowers dating back to the late 1990s. We take pride in having helped build the FTD/Proflowers brand, supplying premium-quality tulips, lilies, iris, and other flowers, including mixed bouquets.

Over the past several years, we have witnessed a decline in business from FTD/Proflowers, yet we have remained a loyal supplier-partner throughout. In recent days, we've become aware of the organizational restructuring at FTD, including downsizing measures aimed at positioning the company for new investment.

While we do not know what specific strategic steps are being considered, these kinds of restructurings are often accompanied by reengineering of the capital and debt structure. I do not want to see our company, and our decades-long relationship, become an unintended casualty of this process. And I presume neither do you.

As of today, your company's outstanding balance with us stands at $3,131,666.25, which includes shipments from March, April, and May. Let me be crystal clear, receiving these funds is absolutely crucial to the continued operation of Sun Valley.

Despite numerous attempts by our staff to reach your team regarding payment, we have not received a response. The last payment we received was on May 9th.

Throughout our 20-year relationship, we have been repeatedly told by FTD/Proflowers representatives that Sun Valley is a valued and key supplier. I presume you share that sentiment. In recent months, various members of your team made verbal commitments that

FTD/Proflowers was "good for the money" and that we would be paid in full, no matter what. In good faith, and based on those assurances, we continued to ship truckload after truckload of flowers for Mother's Day.

As a fellow business leader, I urge you to use your executive authority to direct the immediate payment of $2,959,483.56, which is the balance covering March, April, and the Mother's Day shipments, by wire no later than Monday morning.

For Sun Valley to continue supplying FTD/Proflowers with the quality and consistency your customers expect, this payment is urgent, and it is vital. The livelihoods of 700 hard-working team members and their families depend on your willingness to act.

Looking ahead, Sun Valley is uniquely positioned to support FTD's renewed strategy of leveraging third-party fulfillment partners. We have a proven track record, including the shipment of over 173,000 boxes in a single week for Mother's Day. We have the capacity, infrastructure, and commitment to help FTD succeed in its next chapter.

I trust that you will receive this message in the spirit it is intended. I am confident that your compassion, understanding, and leadership will help ensure that our companies continue this long-standing partnership.

Thank you for your time and attention.

Sincerely,
Lane DeVries
CEO, The Sun Valley Group

In retrospect, the letter I wrote that weekend was all in vain. On Monday, June 3, 2019, FTD filed for bankruptcy.

That morning, CNBC reported:

> FTD Companies stated Monday it has filed for bankruptcy, succumbing to about $200 million in debt the flower and gift delivery company took on to buy Proflowers in 2014. Buying its rival was a move it had hoped would fend off industry change.
>
> At the time of the deal, Proflowers directly sourced its flowers, allowing it to offer similar products for less. Seeing the new model as a threat, FTD acquired Proflowers. But FTD was unable to fully integrate the two companies. Its goals of consolidated technological investments and combining business and marketing teams never fully came to fruition.
>
> "While FTD struggled to unify their businesses and implement the Provide acquisition, the floral industry, and consumer expectation , continued to evolve," CEO Scott Levin testified in documents filed Monday with the bankruptcy court.
>
> FTD has a deal to sell Proflowers and the rest of its North America and Latin America business to an affiliate of private equity firm Nexus Capital for $95 million.

When I heard the horrific news that morning, I nearly fainted. It wasn't just the shock of the bankruptcy. We also had unsold flowers that had been discarded because FTD's Mother's Day orders had come in far lower than they had led us to expect. And now, on top of that, we had over $3 million tied up in the FTD bankruptcy.

According to the court filing in the Delaware Bankruptcy Court dated June 2, 2019, Sun Valley was listed among the 30 largest unsecured creditors, the third-largest overall, with a claim of $3,155,966. We were surpassed only by UPS, at $23.2 million, and Alorica, a temp staffing agency, at $5.2 million.

Among the top 12 creditors, four were flower companies. In addition to

Sun Valley, the list included Elite ($1.9 million), Golden Flowers (Queens) ($1.3 million), and Holex (the Dutch Flower Group) ($800,000). What a dubious distinction, to be the largest floral creditor in this group. I'm sure it was painful for the others as well, but they were billion-dollar giants. For Sun Valley, a much smaller player by comparison, this hit was devastating. It threw our company into a tailspin and marked yet another major setback in our journey.

After the bankruptcy, we continued selling to the new company that had acquired parts of the FTD/Proflowers business out of the bankruptcy estate. But the volumes were a shadow of what they had once been, minimal compared to the two decades prior.

It's important to understand the infrastructure we had built to support those peak volumes. In the flower business, a typical holiday sales multiple is around five times the average weekly volume. But with Proflowers, it was a multiple of more than twenty. For instance, for the entire year 2014, we shipped over 1.2 million bouquets, but more than a million of those were shipped out in the weeks leading up to Valentine's Day and Mother's Day. That kind of surge required enormous planning, labor, cooler space, and logistics capacity.

The Proflowers era taught us a lot. We had always tried to be prudent, ensuring that no single customer became too dominant in our sales mix. At its peak in 2009, Proflowers represented 20.9% of our overall revenue. By 2018 it was down to 12.2%. On paper, we had managed the risk.

But in practice, when they fell, we still got hurt badly. The financial hit, the leftover inventory, and the emotional toll all added up. In hindsight, the FTD bankruptcy became another nail in the coffin of Sun Valley's eventual demise.

CHAPTER 21

OUR BACKS AGAINST THE WALL

All right, they're on our left, they're on our right, they're in front of us, they're behind us… They can't get away this time.

LIEUTENANT COLONEL LEWIS B. (CHESTY) PULLER

B y the summer of 2019, we were truly with our backs against the wall. The financial blow from the FTD/Proflowers collapse was just the latest in a series of hits, landing at a time when our company was already in a precarious position. By October, the bank was preparing to call our loan, and we were scrambling to pull a rabbit out of the hat.

On December 31, 2019, we entered into an agreement with STORE Capital through what's known as a sale-leaseback arrangement. Honestly, I hated every part of this new financial structure, but we had no choice but to acquiesce.

Under the terms of the deal, STORE purchased all of our land in Oxnard, the main facility in Arcata, and the 40-acre Willow Creek Shore farm, then leased it back to the company. All the property improvements (greenhouses and buildings) were financed with a mortgage which was also held by STORE. The biggest challenge with this arrangement was the lack of flexibility. We could not sell or dispose of any underperforming farmland unless we were able to completely take STORE out altogether. This would prove to be a heavy burden in the years to come.

Meanwhile, a line of credit and a $5 million term loan were financed through a separate financial institution. That loan was secured with our inventory, accounts receivable, and the Simpson property (ALC) as collateral. Both finance companies required the company to carry extremely high property valuations for insurance purposes, which caused our insurance premiums to skyrocket.

As 2020 began, I looked at the road ahead and had a hard time seeing how we could navigate the ship under the weight of all these new financial constraints.

Just ten weeks later, the pandemic broke out.

I'll never forget the moment, one Saturday afternoon, with barely an hour's notice, we received an email from a major U.S. supermarket chain requesting an emergency all-vendor floral call. I happened to be walking the fields in Willow Creek at the time. I joined the conference call, along with more than 100 other vendors.

The floral director got right to the point. All purchase orders in the system were canceled, effective immediately. Even product already in transit was instructed to turn around and return to the farm. One vendor asked, "Until what date is this in effect?" The answer was until April 15, which meant through Easter, one of the biggest floral holidays of the year.

Then came the abrupt ending: *"We can't take any more questions. Please send us an email. This is the end of the call. Have a nice day!!"* Click. I stood there in the field, stunned, phone in hand, trying to process what had just happened.

And it wasn't just that customer. Another major account held a similar call that same week. Most wholesalers across the country shut down entirely due to the pandemic. A few retailers, Walmart, Trader Joes, and Albertsons among them, did their best to continue working with us, but the volumes they could take were much restricted.

Meanwhile, millions of flowers were left blooming in our greenhouses and fields with nowhere to go. It was a heartbreaking sight.

In the midst of the COVID period, just as business was beginning to pick back up, we were hit with another unpleasant surprise.

On Saturday, August 1, 2020, while I was driving to the farm at 5:45 a.m., I received a call from our operations team. *Farmnet*, our homegrown software system, was down. That had happened before. Typically, it just required a quick reset from our IT department, and we'd be back in business.

But when I arrived at the office and connected my laptop, I immediately knew something was very wrong. Right before my eyes, I watched as all the information on my screen began getting encrypted. I yanked the laptop from its cradle, powered it down, and called IT.

You guessed it, we had become the victim of a cyberattack.

Unbeknownst to us, starting the previous night, cybercriminals had infiltrated our system and encrypted our entire database. Shortly thereafter, they sent a message to our IT manager demanding a ransom of $7 million in exchange for the decryption key that would unlock our data.

We immediately contacted the FBI and, through our insurance provider, were referred to a cybersecurity firm on the East Coast that specializes in ransomware attacks. They deployed stronger virus protection measures and began negotiations with the cyber criminals.

Eventually, the ransom was reduced to $100,000, payable in Bitcoin, just to regain access to our own data. We agreed. But even after paying, the damage was already done.

Our IT team worked around the clock through the weekend in an attempt to get our inventory and sales systems back online by Monday morning. Despite their efforts, the attack had done serious damage to our database. Some files were recovered. Others were lost forever.

The effects of COVID rippled through every corner of our business throughout 2020. In May 2020, we were forced to make a dreadful but necessary decision to close the Oxnard operation in an effort to curb mounting losses.

In Arcata, millions of unpicked flowers were left standing in the greenhouses during the initial shutdowns. As they sat untouched, mold spores took hold in the soil, leading to disease issues that affected the next crop, particularly in the *Royals* grown in the hoophouses.

Labor shortages only made things worse. In 2020, the delays in moving crates into greenhouses led to broken sprouts and damaged stems. During the worst periods of the pandemic, we had to scale back the number of tulips going into the greenhouse, but by the summer, we still found ourselves with a large inventory of pre-cooled planted tulips sitting in the coolers. This backlog delayed the end of the season by months, with a significant reduction in recovery rate due to aging product.

We did receive a PPP loan, which temporarily helped with cash flow. However, the calculation for the loan amount only included team members on the direct Sun Valley payroll. It excluded the many contracted team members, such as those employed under the H-2A program. While the funds were helpful, they were not nearly enough. By year's end, the losses from unsold inventory far exceeded the size of the PPP loan.

By November 2020, it looked like we were finally about to catch a break. Voters in Ventura County passed Measure O, legalizing commercial cultivation and distribution of cannabis. It opened the door for the possibility to sell the Oxnard property and pay back the STORE obligation.

Meanwhile, in Humboldt County, where our Arcata farm is located, we discovered a regulatory loophole. The county's cannabis ordinance had inadvertently omitted any acreage cap for industrial-zoned land. Since a portion of the Simpson property was zoned industrial, we saw an opportunity. If we could get the site permitted for cannabis use, we could sell the land and use the proceeds to shore up the company's financial position. Despite rumors and speculation in the local press, we never intended to grow cannabis ourselves.

At the same time, we received an offer on the Pleasant Valley property in Oxnard, an offer that would allow us to repay the full STORE commitment.

It felt like a potential turning point. Escrow was opened in April 2021, and the sale was contingent on us providing an updated conditional use permit.

Working with the County of Ventura, we navigated the permit process and, by October 2021, had finalized the updated conditional use permit. We were finally ready to close escrow.

And then… the funding didn't materialize.

At first, there was talk of minor delays. But those "delays" turned into months of excuses and fantastical stories from the buyer's side. Despite our hopes, and countless reassurances, the deal never closed. In the end, there was no funding. What followed over the next three years could fill several pages with tales of empty promises.

In Arcata, we began receiving serious offers from cannabis growers eager to purchase the Simpson property, provided we could secure the necessary cannabis permits. The Humboldt County Planning Department was fully supportive of the project, which proposed cannabis cultivation on 20 acres of industrial-zoned land. The planning director even noted that former industrial sites like this were ideal locations for such developments.

We were well on our way. The process was moving forward, and it looked like this sale might finally help stabilize our finances. But once the County issued notices to neighbors in the immediate area, everything changed.

What followed was an onslaught of opposition, largely driven by a small but vocal group of neighbors. In spring 2021, the project came before the Humboldt County Planning Commission, which approved it. But the opposition appealed, pushing the matter to the Board of Supervisors.

Unlike the strong support we had received back in 1998 during our greenhouse project, this time was very different. The tone of opposition was hostile, and it had a profound influence on the Board. What might have been a straightforward process became entangled in community politics and fear-driven rhetoric.

After more than six hours of hearings over two sessions, the Board ultimately granted us approval, but for 6.8 acres, and more importantly with a long list of burdensome conditions that rendered the project practically unsellable.

And then, in 2022, the bottom dropped out of the cannabis market. In the end, despite all the effort, approvals, and negotiations, this land never fulfilled its intended purpose. The property was never sold, and yet another lifeline for the company slipped away.

We had done the work. We had found buyers. We were granted the approvals, sometimes after months of grueling public hearings. But again and again, we were met with delays, disappointments, or shifting circumstances that pulled the rug out from under us at the last moment.

And all the while, we were still carrying the burdens left by the immigration nightmare, the Proflowers bankruptcy, the cyberattack, and the financial hangover of COVID-19. We were fighting battles on multiple fronts, operational, regulatory, and emotional.

Each time we got close, hope would rise. And each time a solution fell through, the toll on our team, and on me personally, grew heavier. These near-misses didn't just impact the balance sheet. They slowly chipped away at our resilience, as we tried to navigate the company through increasingly narrow channels with fewer and fewer options.

CHAPTER 22

CALAMITIES GALORE

*I have told you these things, so that in me you
may have peace. In this world you will have trouble.
But take heart! I have overcome the world.*

JOHN 16:33

Both personally and professionally, 2021 had its share of calamities, starting with my own health. I was diagnosed with prostate cancer. In 2020 my PSA measurement was 22, and just six weeks later it had climbed to 31. A biopsy revealed high Gleason scores, indicating an aggressive carcinoma. In mid-February I underwent a prostatectomy at UCSF in San Francisco. After a two-week recovery, I was back in the saddle, partly to deal with the commotion stirred up by neighbors over the upcoming hearings on the cannabis project. Full recovery, however, took a while longer.

After the surgery, the pathology report indicated cancer had spread outside the prostate, and also revealed a condition called intraductal carcinoma, which increases the odds of recurrence.

When my PSA began to rise again in the summer of 2021, I made a drastic change to my lifestyle. I adopted a fully plant-based, no processed-foods diet. No pasta, no wheat, no bread, no cereal, no baked products, no deep-fried food, no dairy products, no meat, no fish, no alcohol, no coffee, no sugar, and no salt. Three times a day I had a fresh-pressed juice made from celery, carrots, cilantro, and dandelion leaves. I had a salad for breakfast, lunch and dinner, accompanied with eating nuts. For dinner, in addition to the salad, I had steamed vegetables with beans, quinoa, or brown rice.

Following surgery, UCSF had also conducted a genomic test to assess the likelihood of cancer recurrence. Unfortunately, my score was in the 98th percentile, meaning that 98% of men had a lower chance of recurrence, and only 2% had a higher one. That was not the score I had hoped for. But I was determined to beat the odds with discipline and my new, rigorous diet.

I read extensively on the subject and explored alternative therapies. I began drinking Essaic tea twice a day and even self-administered increasingly high doses of mistletoe. Throughout, I stayed in close contact with my urologist and radiologist, regularly monitoring my PSA levels to ensure they remained in check. I followed this regimen for three years.

. . .

When the first tulip bulb shipments from New Zealand started arriving in the spring of 2021, problems were looming. The Customs and Border Protection (CBP) and USDA inspection station in San Francisco rejected four containers of tulip bulbs because they detected certain bulb mites.

According to the *Encyclopedia of Entomology*, there are 73 known species of *Rhizoglyphus*, commonly referred to as bulb mites. The most common in the U.S. are *Rhizoglyphus echinopus* and *Rhizoglyphus robini*, both of which are omnipresent and considered non-quarantine pests. However, the remaining species on that list are classified as quarantine pests by the USDA.

The issue we encountered was that in the tulip shipments the mites were still in the egg stage, making it impossible for inspectors to determine the exact species. If a local inspector at the San Francisco inspection station couldn't confidently identify the mites as *R. echinopus* or *R. robini*, they were classified as "unknown," and the entire container was automatically rejected. This caused immense consternation, leading to a series of phone calls with both local inspectors and USDA officials in Washington, D.C., to no avail.

A few weeks later, two additional containers from another New Zealand tulip supplier were rejected, this time for a different reason. The wooden bins used to ship the bulbs lacked the proper heat stamp required for entry into the U.S. Ironically, the same bins had already been shipped to tulip growers on the East Coast without any issue. These two containers held 1.2 million red tulip bulbs that we desperately needed for Christmas flowering.

In a scramble to salvage the situation, we were prepared to send two truckloads of compliant bins, a bin dumper, and two team members to the San Francisco CBP inspection station to swap out the bins on-site.

By the time we finally received clearance, five weeks had passed. The bulbs had been held the entire time in containers powered by diesel gensets in the inspection yard. What we didn't realize at the time was that the diesel exhaust had released ethylene gas, which slowly poisoned the bulbs inside. When flowering started, only 5% of the crop was viable.

. . .

On May 14, 2021, the container ship *NYK Delphinus* experienced an engine fire, approximately 50 miles off the coast of Monterey. The ship had to be towed to the Port of Oakland. As fate would have it, we had five containers of lily bulbs, mostly Oriental lilies, on that very vessel.

Even though the ship eventually reached Oakland harbor, our containers were not permitted to be offloaded. At the time, we had no idea why. Then, two weeks later, the owners of the ship declared "*General Average.*"

In my 38 years of importing bulbs from overseas, I had never encountered a "*General Average*" situation before. It's a long-established principle of maritime law, dating back to 1906, which states:

All parties whose goods were saved must contribute proportionally to the losses of those whose goods were sacrificed during a common peril.

In other words, all cargo owners on the ship share in the loss. It also means no cargo can be released until every shipper consents to the terms. We signed our consent agreement right away, hoping to get our containers released as quickly as possible. We wanted those bulbs in our own coolers as soon as we could get them.

Unfortunately, the process of gathering consent from all shippers took months. During that time, the consequences of the engine room fire became clear. The fire had knocked out electricity on the ship for an undisclosed period, which meant the cooling systems had failed. Our bulbs had thawed and, in many cases, had already started to sprout.

At some point during the extended "*General Average*" waiting period, power was restored, and the refrigeration came back online. Thus the lilies were frozen back in again.

By the time our containers were finally released in September, it was too late. Those five containers represented 1.1 million bulbs. An inspection revealed that 700,000 were complete mush. We planted the remaining 400,000 as quickly as possible, hoping for the best. But the results in the greenhouse were dismal.

In the end, we filed a $688,000 insurance claim. However, because the claim fell under a "*General Average*" declaration, only a portion was paid. It could take years to recover the remainder.

* * *

In the aftermath of the pandemic, global container traffic was severely disrupted. Ports along the West Coast were overwhelmed, with massive delays and dozens of container ships idling offshore waiting to be offloaded.

Just before the tulip bulb shipping season began in September, the Port of Oakland made a surprising decision. It would no longer accept container ships arriving from Europe. Instead, all European cargo had to be offloaded in Los Angeles.

This shift caused immediate ripple effects. The Port of LA was already congested, and now it faced a severe shortage of both trucks and chassis. We were suddenly forced to truck our containers from Los Angeles to Arcata, a much longer haul.

Previously, the cost to truck a container from Oakland to Arcata was around $1,200 and from LA to Arcata, it was $2,500. But with trucks in such short supply, the freight companies saw an opportunity and took full advantage. Prices soared to $6,000 per container. It felt like highway robbery, but we had no other choice.

That fall, we shipped more than 100 containers through LA. Compared to previous years, this rerouting alone added more than $480,000 in extra trucking costs.

In addition to the LA rerouting, we also shipped 50 containers through New York and Norfolk. These were offloaded on the East Coast, and the contents were then trucked across the country to Arcata. It was a costly option, about $9,500 per container, but with West Coast transit times stretching to 70 days, this was the only way to get bulbs into the ground early enough for January and Valentine's Day flowering.

However, this method came with its own set of challenges. Many times during the reloading process the pallets weren't properly secured. Often when we opened the truck doors in Arcata, bulbs would come rolling out the back. It was a frustrating and expensive way to ship, but our options were limited.

We also experimented with another route, shipping containers through Montreal, sending them by rail across Canada to Vancouver, and then trucking them down to Arcata, after first being offloaded at our colleagues' facility, Washington Bulb Farms in Mt. Vernon, Washington. It was a convoluted path, but growers in the Pacific Northwest were using this route, and we figured diversifying across three different pathways was a good way to hedge our bets.

Then, in late November, a massive storm hit British Columbia and wiped out parts of the East-West railway. You guessed it, our containers were en route from Montreal to Vancouver when the washout occurred. The shipments had to be rerouted all the way back to Toronto and sat in a holding yard for over a month. They didn't arrive in Arcata until mid-January. Not surprisingly, the bulbs that went through this ordeal did not perform well in the greenhouse later that season.

. . .

The surgery I underwent in 2021 left a deeper mark than I expected. It shook the illusion of invincibility I had carried for so long. For the first time, I felt a real urgency to find a strong second-in-command, someone who could eventually take the reins from me if needed.

We launched an executive search, and found the ideal candidate in Ed Lozano. Ed had previously managed operations in Miami for a large floral importer, and for the past 20 years he had served as General Manager at Sunshine Floral in Oxnard, a bouquet maker partnered with a pompom and gerbera farm. Sunshine Floral had recently closed its doors.

Ed came to Arcata for an interview, and we connected right away. His depth of experience was exactly what we needed. He started by managing the warehouse, but over time his responsibilities expanded to include all postharvest operations. Eventually, Ed became General Manager of the Arcata farm. We complemented each other remarkably well, so much so that I often found myself wishing I had met him ten years earlier.

Then, in November 2022, Ed began not feeling well. A visit to the doctor led to an immediate hospital admission with signs of pneumonia. What followed was a heartbreaking series of hospital stays, and finally, a diagnosis of throat cancer. From that point on, his life became a relentless cycle of hospitals, treatments, and pain. Chemotherapy didn't work. Radiation failed. Multiple surgeries were required to insert tubes into his digestive system. It was agonizing to watch someone so capable, so full of life, be reduced to a shadow of himself.

Throughout 2023, our HR Director and I visited Ed almost daily, either at the hospital or at his home. We watched his health deteriorate, but we also witnessed his incredible courage. Ed passed away the day after Thanksgiving 2023. His long and painful struggle was finally over. Ed, rest in peace my friend. You left a mark on this company, and on me personally. You were more than a second-in-command, you were a partner, a steady hand, a voice of reason, and a man I came to deeply admire.

With Ed's passing, not only did we lose a great leader, but I also lost the dream of a future I had begun to count on. A dream where I could step back, knowing things were in capable hands. That dream vanished when Ed did.

• • •

By 2023, just as we were recovering from the chaos of previous years, the bulb mite issue reared its ugly head again. As the first containers started arriving from New Zealand, the USDA and CBP inspectors began rejecting shipments. By the end of the New Zealand shipping season, nine containers had been turned away over the same unresolved issue, which was the inspector's inability to determine the species of *Rhizoglyphus* mites detected in the bulbs.

In many cases, the mites were still in the egg stage and couldn't be properly identified. If they couldn't be confirmed as *Rhizoglyphus echinopus* or *R. robini*, the two species considered acceptable, the entire container was rejected out of caution. This issue, which had now disrupted two of the last three seasons, became a significant burden to our company and made planning a tulip program using bulbs from the Southern Hemisphere extremely difficult.

In the 2023 season alone we were short nearly five million bulbs because of these rejections. Our New Zealand suppliers, who also had operations in Holland, redirected the rejected containers to Europe and used the bulbs in their own flower programs. For us, it was a major setback. In some cases, entire varieties were missing. In others, the color mixes were thrown off, making it hard to meet customer expectations.

We didn't face this kind of issue with bulbs coming from Holland. That's because since 1952, Dutch bulb exporters organization and the USDA have maintained a preclearance program. During the shipping season, USDA inspectors are stationed in Holland to inspect the bulbs *before* they're loaded into containers. This collaboration ensures clarity and consistency and avoids the kind of uncertainty that plagued our New Zealand imports.

The Dutch preclearance program eliminates the need for bulb shipments to be inspected upon arrival in the U.S., a major advantage when timing and quality are so critical. For years, we had encouraged our New Zealand bulb suppliers to initiate a similar program. Their response was always the same, and that was the U.S. wouldn't send USDA inspectors to New Zealand because the shipping volume was too small to justify the effort.

But when the full-container rejections resurfaced in 2023, I decided to escalate the issue, and reached out to my contact at Certified American Grown, a trade organization representing U.S. flower farmers. He connected me with the right person at the USDA. I asked whether a pre-inspection program for New Zealand tulip bulbs was even possible.

To my surprise, her response was clear and encouraging, *"We can totally do that."* She explained that USDA inspectors are already stationed in New Zealand during the Southern Hemisphere fall for apple inspections destined for the U.S., and said a bulb program could be added. She encouraged the bulb exporters to reach out directly and begin the dialogue. That said, she also warned that setting up such a program would likely take several years.

Ironically, instead of collaborating to solve the problem, our New Zealand suppliers chose a different route. Ahead of the next shipping season, they changed their terms. They would now only ship bulbs if paid in full, in advance, transferring all shipping and importation risk to us. This, despite the fact that they had never seriously pursued a preclearance solution and the mites causing all the trouble originated from their farms.

Historically, these suppliers had offered 90-day terms. Now, we were expected to pay before the bulbs even left New Zealand, shifting our cash flow by 120 to 150 days. It was a frustrating turn, one that placed all the financial exposure on our side, even though the root of the problem had never been properly addressed.

What was ironic is that we had helped these very same suppliers two decades earlier, back when fall tulips from the Southern Hemisphere were a novelty. At the time, they had come knocking on our door, begging if we could help them push fall tulips into the U.S. marketplace. Now, years later, the tables had turned, and the goodwill and trust we had once extended seemed all but forgotten.

. . .

In October 2017, a massive wildfire fueled by strong winds burned down 5,000 houses in Santa Rosa Ca and the surrounding area. The (Tubbs) fire consumed 37,000 acres. A year later, the town of Paradise Ca, located in the Sierra foothills, was mostly burned to the ground and nearly 19,000 structures were destroyed, again fueled by strong winds. The above-ground power lines that are ubiquitous in the Pacific Gas & Electric (PG&E) service area were found to be the cause of both fires. PG&E was sued and filed for Chapter 11 bankruptcy in 2019. The settlements that were negotiated amounted to $13.5 billion Since then, PG&E has accelerated its efforts to bury power lines underground.

Since 2021, 1,500 miles of line have been buried. But the $13.5 billion settlement and the cost of burying the lines have had a detrimental effect on electricity prices in California.

Paradise, Calif., fire devastation, 2018

To put this in perspective, Sun Valley's blended cost of electricity in 2000 was 7.6 cents per kWh; this included all charges. By 2024, that blended cost had risen to 18.5 cents per kWh. But here's the real kicker, in the winter months, we grew our Oriental lilies under 430-watt high-pressure sodium lights. Growing without these lights is not an option in Northern California from October through March.

Back in 2000, when the average electricity rate was 7.6 cents, the night rate was only 3.8 cents. That's because most power was generated by gas-powered turbines, nuclear, or hydro sources that operate around the clock. Demand was lower at night, after most people went to bed, and power was abundant and cheaper.

By 2024, things had changed dramatically. With a much higher share of solar and wind in the energy mix, there was now more power available in the middle of the day and less reliance on gas or nuclear generation. As a result, the equation flipped. Power became relatively scarce at night, and rates followed suit. Nighttime electricity rates jumped from 3.8 cents to 21 cents per kWh. Obviously, the impact this had on the cost of growing Oriental lilies during the winter months in Arcata was significant.

. . .

Property tax in the State of California is assessed at 1% of the property's value at the time of purchase. Annual tax increases are capped at no more than 2% until the property is sold. This assessment structure was established in 1978, when 65% of California voters approved Proposition 13. Any dollar spent on improving the property increases the assessed value accordingly. Machinery and other personal property are also taxed, but since machinery depreciates, the assessed value declines proportionately to that depreciation.

As we added greenhouses over the years, the assessed value of the Sun Valley property rose steadily. In 1993, we made the case to the Humboldt County property tax appeals board that greenhouses, like machinery, also depreciate. After discussion, we reached a compromise that the assessed value of greenhouses would follow a depreciation schedule down to 50%, and from that point forward, the assessed value would be frozen at that level. This agreement served us well for many years.

During the years that we grew bulbs, particularly daffodils, there was also a specific property tax assessment applied to the value of the bulbs, a policy outlined in an internal assessor's memo in February 1983.

In 2020, the Humboldt County Assessor's office conducted an audit, during which the auditor re-interpreted the 1983 memo and increased the assessment for all bulbs planted at our Arcata farm. The methodology outlined in the original memo applied only to bulbs used recurrently, such as daffodils in the 1980s, not to bulbs used only once for cut flower production. The auditor argued that since these bulbs *could* be used for recurrent planting, they were therefore assessable. To make matters worse, he also claimed that bulbs still in transit, on the boat, were subject to assessment as well.

This new interpretation resulted in our annual property tax assessment increasing by more than $200,000. I called several fellow growers who also produced flowers from bulb crops to see if they had faced the same issue. Every one of them said their respective county assessors did not include bulb value in the property assessment. We hired a property tax attorney to explore options for protest, but we learned that under California law the 60-day appeal window had already passed, leaving us with little recourse. In our final year of operations, we were assessed over $770,000 in property taxes. It was yet an additional burden on an already financially stressed enterprise.

There were moments when I seriously began to wonder if this was simply no longer meant to be. Everything we had worked so hard for seemed to be unraveling faster than we could hold it together. I remember sitting alone, asking myself, *what is the purpose of all this?*

I caught myself thinking that maybe God had another plan in mind, because this clearly wasn't it. It felt like every door seemed to be closing, and every step forward was met with another setback. And in that quiet, painful uncertainty, the soul searching was running deep.

CHAPTER 23

ALL THINGS ADDING UP

The last straw that broke the camel's back.

ORIENTAL PROVERB

The myriad number of issues described in the previous pages culminated in shrinking margins. Stacked on top of a series of unfortunate events, this pushed the company deeper into debt. We eventually found ourselves having to deal with hard money lenders. One such lender charged a staggering 15% interest, and during the COVID crisis, that rate increased to a default rate of 18%, eventually climbing to 21%.

Several people I spoke with questioned whether these interest rates were even legal. In many states across the country, "usury" laws are in place to protect borrowers from predatory interest rates. But, as you may have guessed, in the state of California, certain financial institutions are exempt from these laws. That meant there was no legal limit to how high our lender could push the interest rate.

Developments in automation in Holland for growing tulips had taken on a whole new dimension. By 2024, 85% of tulips grown there were produced hydroponically, grown in water, mostly on rolling tables, with robots handling the planting. We closely followed these advancements, but to our chagrin there was little we could do in terms of capital investment to keep pace with the rapid progress.

We estimated that upgrading our tulip operation to meet this new standard of automation would require an investment of $10 million. That was money we simply didn't have; we were barely keeping our heads above water. Once you're behind the curve, it becomes nearly impossible to catch up. Instead, with labor rates continuing to climb and our facilities aging, a growing share of our cost of goods sold was going toward labor and repair & maintenance.

Some folks might say, "Why didn't you just raise your prices?" Let me tell you, that is easier said than done. In such a competitive environment, raising prices often meant losing business. Let me give you an example. With the rising cost of growing Oriental lilies, we raised our price by 5% to a particular supermarket chain we had been supplying for more than 30 years. The next thing we knew, their corporate office issued a request for proposal (RFP) for a range of flower types, including Oriental lilies.

As part of the RFP process, they introduced a brand-new box specification, mandating a fixed number of bunches per box. When we received a sample of this new box, it was immediately clear that our lilies didn't come close to fitting. When we pointed this out to our contact at the chain, the response was, "The other growers had no trouble fitting their lilies in the box." That certainly was a clue. They also mentioned that our price was 20% higher than the competition.

Our lilies were larger, that's why they didn't fit in the new box. The customer threatened to pull the business based on the quotes we had submitted. This wasn't an idle threat; they had already taken some divisions away in the past. At this point, the division buyer got involved directly and told us that if we agreed to keep the price the same as last year, we could continue supplying that division.

Ultimately, we acquiesced. Losing another division would have been devastating, especially with crops already in the pipeline, plants growing in the greenhouse and bulbs sitting in the cooler. (The typical production cycle is 18 to 20 months from ordering bulbs to harvesting the last flowers.) So there we were, pressured by the fear of losing the business, coerced into holding prices steady, and watching our margins get squeezed even further.

Others might say, "Why don't you just shrink your production?" We did start doing that, but it came with unintended consequences. The large facility we had built over the years was designed to handle a certain volume, and as production declined, the cost per unit rose. Simply put, we had a big machine, and running less product through it made everything more expensive.

Another challenge with lower volumes was that production dips, caused by weather, for example, still had to be navigated while meeting customer commitments. Walmart, in particular, had a punitive policy; if orders weren't filled at 100%, it triggered sizable fines. The irony of the situation was that our wholesale customers who paid higher prices would be deprived of product during these low-supply times to avoid paying penalties to some mass market customers.

It became a recurring theme, with supermarket chains demanding more control, tighter compliance, and putting pressure on prices, while leaving growers to shoulder all the risk. The balance of power had shifted. At one time, we had partnered with retailers in a way that felt mutually beneficial. But over time, the dynamics evolved into something far less collaborative. The mass market buyers held the leverage, and growers, despite carrying the operational, financial, and seasonal risks, were left with razor-thin margins and little flexibility.

This growing imbalance between mass market power and supplier viability was frustrating and unsustainable. It felt like a slow squeeze that left little room to breathe.

· · ·

By the spring of 2023, we had come to the sobering conclusion that we could no longer shoulder the financial burden on our own. A capital infusion or a buyer would be the only viable path forward.

We engaged an investment broker with experience in the nursery sector. They assembled a detailed prospectus and began reaching out to private equity firms and potential strategic buyers. But unlike the wave of enthusiasm sparked by a similar effort 23 years earlier, this time the market response was muted. Shrinking margins deterred most of the private equity firms they contacted.

We did enter discussions with a number of strategic buyers, those who understood the long-term potential of the business, especially if supported by a meaningful capital expenditure program. By September 2023, one consortium, made up of a domestic and an international floral company, moved forward and drafted a purchase agreement.

But the optimism was short-lived. Within 40 days, it became clear that bank financing for the deal would be problematic. The group rescinded their offer.

To make matters worse, in October 2023, our New Zealand tulip suppliers informed us of new payment terms for the upcoming season, requiring advance payment and shifting more financial risk onto us. This only compounded the company's already strained liquidity.

After fifteen years of holding things together following the 2008 immigration nightmare, fighting with everything I had to keep the company alive, I finally paused to take stock of the road ahead. By October 2023, the writing was on the wall. In conversations with my partners, we came to a painful but clear conclusion that in the absence of a serious buyer or investor to help revive the company, we saw no other solution but to initiate an orderly wind down.

The tulip and iris bulbs from Holland were already in transit, so we committed to finishing out that cycle. But the lilies were a different story.

We had purchased only a minimal quantity of lily bulbs for the upcoming season. The fall 2023 lily harvest in Holland had been a disaster. Persistent rains made field access difficult, and many growers struggled to dig their lily bulb crops. Exporters were rejecting water-damaged bulbs left and right, and some fields were left untouched because they were simply too wet to harvest. As a result, availability was tight, and prices were climbing.

When I informed our lily suppliers that we were scaling back our program, it caught them off guard. But given the eager lily market and short supply, they were able to place our reserved bulbs elsewhere without difficulty.

It was critical to keep the wind-down strategy strictly confidential. Had word leaked out prematurely, we risked losing both customers and key team members. I vividly remember another flower grower in California who announced in the fall of 2023 that he would cease operations after Valentine's Day 2024. The response was swift and brutal. Customers immediately shifted their orders elsewhere, and much of his Valentine's crop ended up blooming out in his greenhouses, unsold.

We were determined to avoid that scenario. Keeping our plans under wraps wasn't easy, but it was essential. The Northern Hemisphere tulip bulb season would carry us through to the end of July. The same applied to the iris program. We also had enough Royal bulb stock from the previous year's crop to produce flowers into late summer.

As for the Oriental lilies, our inventory would carry us through May. To maintain appearances and avoid raising concern among the team, we purchased a few additional containers and continued weekly plantings. It was a careful dance, sustaining production while preparing for closure, all without tipping our hand.

To navigate the complexities of an orderly closure, we brought in a wind-down expert to guide us through each phase of the process. We also retained legal counsel to ensure full compliance with all regulatory and contractual obligations. Some advisors on the team suggested we simply throw in the towel, file for bankruptcy, and walk away. But I was vehemently opposed to that idea.

For more than four decades we had built relationships with many of our vendors, some of whom had stood by us through thick and thin. The easy path might have been to walk away, but that would have betrayed the very values that had guided this company from the beginning. I had seen what happened when others in our industry took that route. Suppliers were left badly wounded, trust was destroyed, and the ripple effects lingered for years.

We had felt the sting ourselves, Proflowers being the most recent and painful example.

But *The Pursuit of Purpose* isn't just a title, it's been the compass by which we've navigated every decision. Even in this final chapter, that purpose meant doing the right thing, even when it wasn't the easiest. With viable crops still in our greenhouses and coolers, we had real value we could recover. After the Mother's Day sales and with a solid accounts receivable balance, we paid off as many vendors as we possibly could. We wholeheartedly tried to close the business with integrity.

We couldn't afford to wait much longer to make the announcement due to the 60-day requirement under the WARN Act, which obligated us to provide notice and continue payroll during that period, a significant financial commitment. At the same time, we were still in conversations with potential buyers and investors. On May 21, we informed the bank of our decision to begin the wind down and that the WARN Notices would be issued the following day. On May 22, 2024, we convened a special farm meeting where I personally explained the situation to the entire team.

· · ·

Within weeks, the same company that had made an offer the previous September resurfaced. They reengaged in conversations with both banks and began making tangible progress, negotiating a price for the Arcata real estate as well as the equipment. It seemed that, even at this late stage, a deal might still come together. During our discussions, the buyer asked how many tulip bulbs we had secured for the upcoming season. While the number was modest compared to previous years, it was still a meaningful amount.

Meanwhile, the tulip bulb harvest in Holland turned out to be the worst crop in sixty years. The same persistent wet weather that disrupted the lily harvest in the fall of 2023 had continued through winter. Entire fields of tulips drowned from excessive rain, and by digging time, the crop was down by 30% from expectations. Bulbs were nearly impossible to obtain, and those available fetched prices double or even triple what they had been just a few years earlier.

Even though we had reached agreement on the company's purchase price, the potential buyer made the availability and skyrocketing cost of tulip bulbs the pivotal issue. That's when it became crystal clear to me that God had other plans.

What were the odds that the worst tulip crop in sixty years would become the breaking point for the buyer's decision to walk away? This couldn't be mere coincidence; it felt like a divine message, telling me it was time to surrender, time to let go. After forty years of pouring my heart and soul into this company, I realized that my purpose might no longer be to fight for its survival, but to trust in a larger plan unfolding.

I had been resisting that premise. After the immigration nightmare in 2008, we did everything we could to put the pieces back together. In my speeches I had rallied the team, to inspire them with a sense of mission, and I believe it mattered. But now, with the path closing in front of me, I began to understand that the purpose I had served through all those years, the purpose of building, guiding, and persevering, was giving way to a new chapter. Even though the adversities were not random, they were shaping something deeper in me, preparing me for this moment of release. It was all part of God's plan.

Despite all the hardship, Sun Valley stood as an iconic company, remarkable not only before 2008, but perhaps even more so in the years that followed. The struggles we endured did not go unnoticed, either in the local community or across the floral industry. Many witnessed our relentless quest not just to survive, but to create a distinct "Sun Valley" identity that was rooted in resilience, innovation, and purpose.

We earned our reputation through excellence in bulb flowers, quality standards, and industry leadership, from box standardization and cold chain innovation to groundbreaking growing techniques and the introduction of new crops such as Ilex and Butterflies. We were known for bold marketing moves, including championing Women's Day as a floral holiday. We were known for our team, a group of ordinary people achieving extraordinary results. Locally, we were recognized for our generosity, supporting fundraisers and churches, and giving countless individuals a second chance through employment.

All of this, every breakthrough, and every act of service, happened not in the absence of struggle, but often because of it. And woven through it all was a clear and unwavering pursuit of purpose.

As I began to let go, it became clear that the legacy of Sun Valley wasn't tied to a balance sheet or a set of greenhouses. It would live on in the impact we made, the values we upheld, and the lives we touched. That realization gave me peace. It reminded me that the pursuit of purpose doesn't end with the closing of a chapter, instead it simply takes a new form. My next steps would be guided not by holding on to what was, but by honoring what we built and finding new ways to live out that same purpose in whatever came next.

After the buyer walked away for the second time, the wind down was now imminent. Following the May 22 announcement, the bank imposed restrictions on what we could pay toward the remaining accounts payable. Still, we did everything we could to honor our commitments, making as many payments as possible within the limits of our approved budget. By August, our credit line was fully paid off, and with the upcoming equipment auction and the sale of the old Simpson property, it still looked promising that we could pay off a term loan and cover all our vendor obligations.

Leading up to the auction, the equipment auctioneer estimated we would see at least $2.8 million in proceeds. The auction began on September 16th and ran for three days. I will never forget those days, but for all the wrong reasons. What unfolded was an utter disaster. Instead of a fair valuation of our assets, it became a grand giveaway.

The day after the auction, a caravan of pickup trucks and trailers rolled onto the property to collect their newly acquired bargains. Some of the buyers were outright rude and unreasonable, which was especially ironic, given the prices they had paid. The pick-up process dragged on for more than a month, leaving behind more than just empty buildings; with it came some deep emotional scars. When it was finally over, the net proceeds totaled less than $800,000.

This was, obviously, a major setback to our plan to pay everyone. With the disappointing auction results, our last remaining hope rested on the sale of the old Simpson property (ALC). But in August 2024, it is hard to comprehend, but yet another blow struck. A portion of the roof on the 400,000 square-foot building came crashing down; roughly 10,000 square feet were affected. While that was a relatively small section of the structure, it left a visible and significant blemish for any potential buyer.

The timing couldn't have been worse. We obtained repair estimates ranging from $1.6 to $2 million, and any interested party immediately factored that into their offer, slashing the property's value. The damage made it far harder to attract serious buyers, and as a result, our hopes of fully clearing all outstanding obligations were cast into doubt once again.

• • •

Meanwhile, on the health front, my PSA continued to rise despite all my efforts. I had followed that rigorous plant-based diet for over three years, with no meat, no dairy, no pasta, no bread, no sugar, no alcohol, and much more, yet the numbers kept creeping upward. Eventually, in the fall of 2024, I had to come to terms with the limits of diet alone and turned back to the Western medical approach. In November, I received my first Lupron injection, a hormone blocker that marked the start of a new chapter in treatment. Then, in December and January, I underwent 38 near-daily radiation treatments.

During the final week of radiation, a severe rash developed on my body, stretching from mid-arm to the bottom of my ribcage on both sides. The itching was surreal. The prescribed creams offered little relief. The rash was excruciating throughout the day and even worse at night, robbing me of sleep and peace. I had three agonizing weeks before the rash finally began to subside. Yet even after that, the relentless itching under my arms and along my sides persisted for another two weeks before it finally eased.

Around that same time, I began noticing that walking uphill around our house was becoming increasingly difficult. I had a tightness in my chest that didn't occur on flat ground, but the discomfort was unmistakable. Then, several nights in a row, I woke up with that same tightness, as if I had just ran several miles. It happened about five times, and each time it felt more alarming. I finally checked in with my doctor, who diagnosed it as an unstable angina. He told me I was at serious risk of a heart attack and needed to go to the hospital immediately.

The next morning, a cardiologist performed a catheterization and discovered two significant blockages, one was 70% in the LAD, commonly referred to as the "windowmaker" artery, and the other was 95% in the OM1. He placed two stents in my left coronary arteries, and I was discharged the next day.

Once again, the Lord had come to my rescue. A major medical disaster had been averted, and I was deeply aware that divine grace had stepped in once more.

In the midst of professional loss, physical pain, and emotional exhaustion, this health scare felt like yet another blow, but also a profound wake-up call. And yet, just like so many times before, I was reminded that I was not walking through this valley alone. The timing of the diagnosis, the precision of the intervention, and the outcome itself felt nothing short of miraculous. It was as if God was saying, "You've given everything, now let Me carry you."

I had surrendered the business, endured the trials of cancer, and now stood face to face with my own mortality. But through it all, there remained a thread of purpose that was refined, but not broken, by adversity. I came to see that this chapter was not about what I could still hold onto, but about what I was being prepared to pass on: the lessons, the values, and the story. It wasn't just about resilience anymore; it was about grace. And in that grace, I found peace.

Looking back, I could never have imagined that the culmination of four decades of work would come with this level of agony, hard choices, and unexpected turns. But I also never imagined how deeply I would come to understand the meaning of purpose, as a thread that runs through every season, every challenge, every act of perseverance.

The collapse of the business, the unraveling of long-held plans, even the breakdown of my body, all of it became part of something greater. I didn't just endure those moments; I was starting to be shaped by them. And in the stillness that followed, I began to see that surrender isn't the end of purpose, it is at that moment that new clarity is born. The legacy of Sun Valley lives on, not only in flowers or fields, but also in the people, the principles, and the pursuit of something bigger than ourselves. That pursuit continues.

CHAPTER 24

PURPOSE JOURNEY

Although no one can go back and make a brand-new start,
anyone can start from now and make a new ending.

CARL BARD

All the experiences, every setback, every painful chapter, only drew me closer to God. I'll never forget after my back issues in 2007 and when the immigration disaster hit us in 2008, my brother said, "Lane, this sounds like the story of Job." I responded somewhat puzzled. "Job? Who's that?" Back then, I barely knew the story. But I've come to know it well since. Job was a man of deep faith, devoted to God, and yet he was tested beyond imagination. In a single day, he lost everything, his livestock, his servants, and worst of all, all of his children. As if that grief weren't enough, he was then struck with a painful skin disease. His suffering was profound, both in body and soul. Even his closest friends turned on him, insisting that he must have sinned, that surely God was punishing him. But Job never gave up on God. He clung to his faith when everything else was stripped away.

That conversation with my brother, comparing my trials in 2007 and 2008 to the story of Job, stuck with me. It sparked something deeper. I had started going back to church several years earlier in 2004, mainly because I wanted Tony and Sarah to grow up with a foundation in Christian values and traditions. Every Sunday we sat in the pews together. I enjoyed the sermons, found comfort in the hymns, and felt a sense of community. But until that moment, I hadn't truly explored the Bible for myself.

The story of Job changed that. It pulled me in. I began reading more, searching for meaning, for perspective, and for strength. What I discovered was profound. The Bible is filled with stories where hardship becomes the very ground on which faith is built. Struggle wasn't the exception, but instead it was the path. Let me share two examples that especially spoke to me.

Take the story of Joseph. He was the favored son of Jacob, which stirred deep jealousy in his brothers. In a moment of betrayal, they sold him into slavery and lied to their father, claiming a wild animal had killed him. In Egypt, Joseph served faithfully in the house of his master, until another injustice struck. The master's wife tried to seduce him, and when Joseph refused, staying true to his principles, she falsely accused him of assault.

For doing the right thing, Joseph was thrown into prison. So much for being faithful, right? Yet even in that dark place, his gift made room for him. When Pharaoh's cupbearer and baker both had troubling dreams, Joseph interpreted them accurately: one would be restored, the other executed. But despite asking to be remembered, Joseph remained forgotten for two more years. Then Pharaoh had a dream no one could explain, and the cupbearer finally spoke up. Joseph was brought before the king, interpreted the dream of a coming famine, and offered a plan. Pharaoh was so impressed, he made Joseph second in command over all Egypt.

Years later, when the famine spread and Jacob's sons came to Egypt seeking food, they unknowingly stood before their long-lost brother, who now was a powerful ruler. What had begun in betrayal and suffering had been transformed into a story of redemption and purpose.

Then there's the powerful story of Saul, later known as the Apostle Paul. Around 40 AD, he was a fierce persecutor of early Christians, determined to silence the growing movement. But everything changed through a miraculous encounter with the risen Lord on the road to Damascus. That moment transformed him. From an enemy of the faith, he became one of its most passionate messengers, dedicating his life to spreading the gospel, especially to the Gentiles.

But Paul's journey was anything but easy. He was stoned by angry mobs who refused to hear his message, beaten with rods three times, and lashed on five occasions, thirty-nine lashes each time. He was shipwrecked three times, once spending an entire day and night adrift in the open sea. He was bitten by a viper, endured hunger and thirst, danger from bandits, and betrayal from those he trusted. And yet, through every trial, Paul never let go of his faith.

His letters, written to believers in places such as Rome, Corinth, Ephesus, and Galatia, are filled not with bitterness or despair, but with gratitude, encouragement, and an unshakable trust in God's grace and purpose.

Reading these stories, Job's endurance, Joseph's redemption, and Paul's unshakable mission, opened my eyes.

Their stories gave me a lens through which to see my own challenges differently, not as punishment, but as preparation. These weren't just biblical figures anymore, they became inspirations on my journey, showing me that adversity doesn't break faith, it actually builds it.

The more I read the Bible, the more I began to see the beauty in how its books are intricately connected, woven together with a single purpose, to lead the reader into a relationship with Jesus Christ. What started as curiosity, sparked by hardship, became a deep and personal faith journey. As the years went by, that relationship with the Lord only grew stronger. Scripture came alive for me, not just as ancient wisdom, but as a living guide. That journey of faith eventually brought me to places I never imagined, even to the pulpit, sharing the good news of hope, redemption, and the power of God's grace. What once felt like hardship became testimony. And what once were trials became steppingstones toward a purpose far greater than I could have written on my own.

As I mentioned earlier, the flame of faith truly began to burn during the drives I made during my regular trips to Canada and back, first from Toronto to our farm in St. Catherines, and from LAX to our farm in Oxnard. Alone in the car, I'd tune in to Christian radio stations and listen to skillful, spirit-filled orators unpack Scripture with clarity and conviction. Their messages stirred something in me. With each mile, I felt God speaking directly into my life, bringing Scripture to life in a way I had never experienced before.

Those quiet times behind the wheel became sacred ground. It was there, in the solitude of the road and the stillness of my heart, that God began to do a deeper work in me. The Word was no longer distant, it was personal, alive, and transformative. That's when the flame became a fire, and faith moved from the sidelines to the center of my life.

For many years, we grew a flower called *Ornithogalum dubium*, often referred to as the orange and yellow version of "Stars of Bethlehem." We sourced the bulbs from a grower in Israel. In March 2011, my wife and I had

Ornithogalum dubium in Israel (2011)

the opportunity to travel there to see firsthand how these "dubiums" were grown. It was a fascinating trip from a horticultural perspective. We spent several days visiting farms and learning about the growing techniques.

But what made the journey truly unforgettable were the days that followed. We visited historic and sacred sites, Nazareth, the Sea of Galilee, the River Jordan, and of course, Jerusalem. To walk the very land where Jesus lived, taught, and performed miracles was deeply moving. It gave the Scriptures a new texture, no longer just words on a page, but places I had now seen and touched.

Since the ancient city of Jerusalem was destroyed by the Romans in 70 AD, most of what stands today has been rebuilt over the centuries. Only fragments of the original structures remain. The most significant remnant of antiquity is the foundation of the Temple, now known as the Wailing Wall, a sacred site of prayer and reflection. In recent years, archaeologists have uncovered ancient streets buried beneath layers of rubble, revealing traces of the old city beneath its current surface.

Ancient Olive trees along the slopes of the Mount of Olives

Just outside the eastern walls of Jerusalem lies the Kidron Valley. From there, the land rises again toward the Mount of Olives. Unlike the city itself, this hillside remained largely untouched by the Roman destruction as there were no buildings to be destroyed. It was, and still is, a quiet slope dotted with ancient olive trees. Nestled among them is the Garden of Gethsemane, a place whose significance is hard to put into words. Some of the olive trees there are believed to be thousands of years old, silent witnesses to the events of that fateful night before Good Friday.

That site had a profound impact on me. I remember sitting in a small chapel nestled among the olive trees, and to my surprise, I began to cry. I'm not someone who cries easily, but in that moment, I couldn't stop the tears. I was overwhelmed by the weight of what had taken place there; this was where Jesus prayed in anguish while His disciples, unable to stay awake, drifted into sleep. This was the place where Judas betrayed Him, where Roman soldiers arrived to arrest Him. Sitting there, I felt an unexplainable connection, intimate, real, almost personal. As the tears rolled down my cheeks, I sensed I was on holy ground.

The tour group had already gathered outside, and at one point, my wife came back into the chapel to gently urge me along. But honestly, I could have stayed there for hours. Something sacred had reached deep into my soul that day.

That visit to Israel only deepened my thirst to learn more; it stirred something that felt like a calling. It laid the foundation for what would become a growing passion to share the Word with others. When we returned home to California, I couldn't wait to tell people about what we had seen and felt. I shared stories from the trip with Dan Price, our pastor at the Eureka Presbyterian Church. He was fascinated, especially since he hadn't yet been to Israel himself. After hearing about our experience, he asked if I'd be willing to share it with the congregation during a Sunday worship service. We had taken plenty of photos, so putting together a presentation would be easy enough.

About a month later, I gave the talk. I shaped it into a kind of mini-sermon, weaving in Scripture and reflections as I went. To my surprise, it was warmly received. People thanked me afterward, not just for the pictures, but for the meaning behind them, for helping them connect the biblical stories with real places and real emotion. That moment opened a new door.

Several years later, in 2015, a member of the Eureka church approached me. She told me that one of their more seasoned leaders was moving out of the area. That woman had occasionally filled in for the pastor and had also been preaching regularly at a small church in Blue Lake, which is just five miles east of Arcata. That little church didn't have a full-time pastor and instead relied on a rotating team of four lay preachers, each taking a turn once a month. With her departure, a vacancy had opened up and they asked if I might be interested in stepping into that role.

My first reaction was, *"Hey, I'm just a flower farmer, not a theologian."* But then thinking about it a little more, I realized it doesn't take a theology degree to share the good news of Jesus Christ. After all, the original disciples were mostly fishermen, and yet they became some of the most effective messengers of the Gospel. The church member who had approached me gently reminded me of the talk I'd given four years earlier about our trip to Israel, and how deeply it had resonated with the congregation. That encouragement stuck with me.

After some prayer and reflection, I decided to give it a try. I figured if the folks at the Blue Lake Church didn't connect with the message, it could simply be a one-time appearance, and that would be that. As it turned out, my first sermon was scheduled for May 10th, 2015, on Mother's Day. In the flower business, Mother's Day is the single busiest event of the year. The three weeks leading up to it are a marathon of long days, typically starting at 5 a.m. and going until 8 p.m. or later, with just enough sleep to do it all over again the next day.

So, when the elder at Blue Lake asked if I could preach on *that* Sunday, I paused. For a moment I thought to myself, *"I must be nuts."* But then I said yes.

During the week leading up to Sunday, I was driving home one evening around 8:15, exhausted from the day, when a wave of panic suddenly hit me: *"This Sunday, I'm giving the sermon, what am I going to say?"* A cold sweat came over me. My first reaction was anxiety, maybe even a bit of regret. But then, something shifted. A quiet voice inside urged me to step back and let the Holy Spirit lead the way. I reached for the radio, flipping through the stations, hoping for some peace, and there it was. I landed on a Christian station, and at that exact moment, Sister Ann Shields was giving a commentary on Acts 10:44–48 and Psalm 98, the very Scripture verses I was assigned to preach on that Sunday. I couldn't believe it. It was as if God Himself had reached through the static to say, *"I've got you."* That moment reiterated what I was learning all along, and that is putting your trust in the Lord always pays off.

I chose a few hymns that aligned with the message, and since it was Mother's Day, we brought flowers and gave them to all the mothers in attendance. It felt like the perfect blend of my two worlds, faith and flowers. When I finished the sermon, something unexpected happened, as the congregation began to clap. Not just polite applause, but warm, enthusiastic appreciation. Their message was clear; they wanted me to come back. And so, I did.

That began a rhythm of monthly sermons that continued for four and one-half years, right up until COVID hit. The little church in Blue Lake closed its doors during the pandemic, and sadly, it never reopened.

Somehow, I had the intuition to record that first sermon on my cell phone, and I kept doing so in the months that followed. Eventually, we compiled the recordings and created a website: *LaneDeVries.com, Sermons by a Flower Farmer.* In time, I also began videotaping some of the sermons and sharing them on Facebook and YouTube, along with an audio version on Spotify and Apple Music. To my surprise, some of the videos on Facebook received more than a thousand views. I never imagined that messages delivered in a tiny church in Blue Lake could reach people far beyond Humboldt County.

In each sermon, I tried to weave in real-life stories from the farm, drawing from the soil, the seasons, the challenges, and blessings of flower growing. Those analogies made Scripture come alive in a tangible way, and someone affectionately dubbed them the "flower farmer parables." The name stuck. Even after the little church in Blue Lake closed during the pandemic, I continued sharing sermons at other churches throughout Humboldt County. It's something I genuinely enjoy, and I've come to see it as a meaningful part of my life's calling. It has been, without a doubt, a powerful contributor to my pursuit of purpose.

The website now has 48 sermons from those four and one-half years. Among the many messages I shared over those years, one seems especially appropriate to include here. It speaks to the themes of renewal, trust, and moving forward even when the path is uncertain. The sermon is called *"A New Beginning."* I share it not just as a reflection of my faith journey, but also as an invitation, to pause, and to reflect.

As I look back on those years in the pulpit, born out of unexpected opportunity, sustained by faith, and fueled by a sense of calling, I'm reminded of how often God plants purpose in places we least expect. What began with a trip to Israel and a hesitant "yes" to a small church sermon eventually became a treasured chapter of my life, one filled with meaning, growth, and purpose.

> *When one door of happiness closes, another one opens,*
> *but often we look so long at the closed door that we*
> *do not see the one which has been opened for us.*
>
> HELEN KELLER

CHAPTER 25

A NEW BEGINNING

For four generations, my family grew tulips in Holland. But that long-standing tradition seemed to come to an end in 1983, when I immigrated to the United States and took a position with a lily-growing company in Oregon.

My brother and father bringing tulips into the greenhouse in 1976 in Holland

But a "new beginning" came in 1984, when I settled in Arcata and began growing tulips once again. We imported two containers of bulbs that fall, and by the spring of 1985, we picked our first harvest. The rest, as they say, is history.

"Speaking of 'A New Beginning,' for years I've been driving a 1997 Ford F250 pickup. That truck has seen a lot: countless trips to Smith River and Willow Creek, even a few all the way down to Oxnard. It's gone through muddy fields, over forest land, and taken its fair share of scratches from overhanging branches. I once tried to squeeze it through a narrow spot at the farm; it didn't quite fit and peeled some paint off the side.

One time, driving back late at night from a 49ers game, I got a little too close to a redwood tree in Richardson Grove and the mirror slammed hard into the door. Another time, a tree came down right on the hood and left a pretty good dent. In other words, that truck has some serious mileage and has seen more than its fair share of abuse. In the spring of 2014, at 5:30 a.m. on a Saturday morning, I was heading to work, coming down Fickle Hill, when I was hit by a drunk driver. It was someone who was just making his way home from a late-night party, driving up the hill.

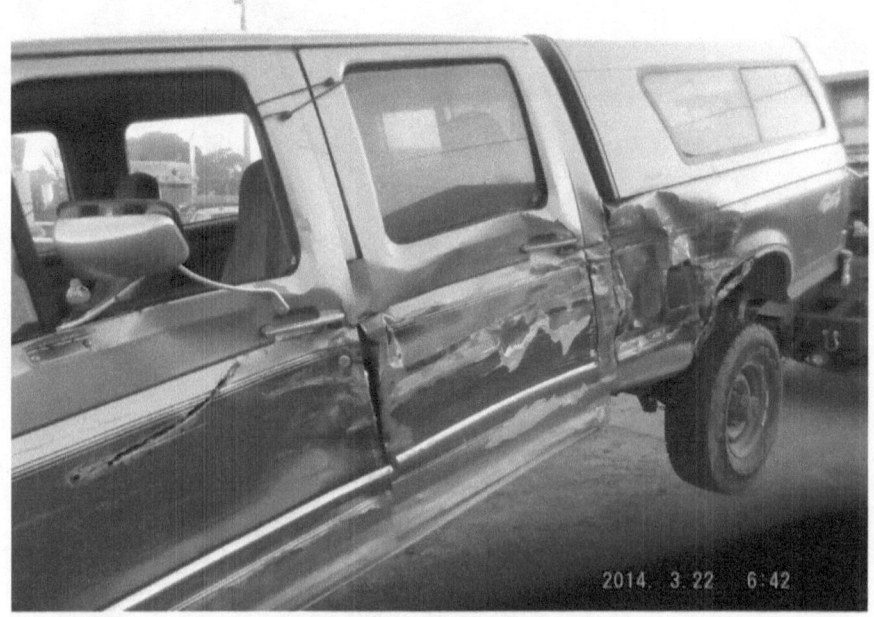

He failed to make a sharp S-turn and slammed into my truck, wiping out the entire left side. After the collision I sat there with shattered glass all over me. The truck was totaled, by all accounts, and that should've been the end of it. It had served me well for 18 years. But we weren't quite ready to say goodbye. We bought it back from the insurance company, salvaged the title, and had it fixed up again.

After a significant overhaul and a fresh coat of paint, that old truck got 'A New Beginning.' After twenty-nine years and 492,000 miles, it's still running on the original engine. The transmission was replaced for the first time at 487,000 miles. People often comment on how good it looks for its age. But let me tell you, it didn't always look like that. It wasn't until it got 'A New Beginning.'

Each early summer, several thousand students graduate from Cal Poly Humboldt and College of the Redwoods. The respective school presidents deliver their commencement addresses. The word 'commencement' connotes a beginning. While these students have completed their formal education, the ceremony marks 'A New Beginning,' the start of the next chapter in their lives

What does the Bible say about new beginnings? Quite a lot, actually. The very first words of Scripture set the tone: '*In the beginning, God created the heavens and the earth*' (Genesis 1:1). In Genesis 9, Noah and his family received *"A New Beginning"* after the great flood, an opportunity to repopulate the earth and walk in covenant with God.

Joseph's story is another powerful example. Sold into slavery by his own brothers, falsely accused, and thrown into prison, it surely looked like the end. But then, after interpreting Pharaoh's dream, he experienced *"A New Beginning"* that elevated him to second in command over all of Egypt.

Four centuries later, Moses faced his own turning point. After killing an Egyptian, he fled into the wilderness, becoming a fugitive in the land of Midian, a desolate corner of the Saudi Arabian desert. Once a powerful prince and likely heir to Pharaoh, Moses was now a shepherd in exile. He must have felt like his life had unraveled. But even there, in isolation and obscurity, God was preparing him for *"A New Beginning,"* a mission that would change the course of history.

The Lord spoke to Moses from the burning bush, and at that moment, he received *"A New Beginning."* What seemed like the end of his story was, in fact, just the turning point. He ultimately became one of the most influential figures in Jewish history, chosen to lead the Israelites out of slavery in Egypt and toward freedom.

Later, Joshua and the Israelites also received *"A New Beginning"* as they crossed the Jordan River into the Promised Land, the land of "milk and honey," after wandering in the wilderness for 40 years.

Jonah didn't want to listen to God; he went his own way. But after being tossed overboard in the middle of a violent storm at sea and spending three days inside a great fish, he was spit out onto the beach. It was there, covered in seaweed and sand, that Jonah received *"A New Beginning."* This time, he obeyed. He went to Nineveh and preached what may have been the shortest sermon ever recorded, yet it sparked what is still considered the greatest revival in human history.

At the farm, we've employed *Teen Challenge* students working part-time. During the busy weeks leading up to Easter and Mother's Day they were a tremendous help. But more than their work ethic, it's their stories that stand out. These are people who have walked through the darkest valleys of life, addiction, brokenness, despair. Yet each one made the decision to surrender their lives to Jesus Christ, and in doing so, they received *"A New Beginning."*

As Paul wrote in 2 Corinthians 5:17: *"This means that anyone who belongs to Christ has become a new person. The old life is gone; a new life has begun!"*

The final *"New Beginning"* is described on the very last page of the Bible, in Revelation 21.

• • •

The writer of the book of Revelation is widely believed to have been the Apostle John, often referred to as *"the disciple whom Jesus loved."* John was part of

Jesus' inner circle. Alongside his brother James and Peter, he was present on the mountain during the Transfiguration, where Jesus stood in glory with Moses and Elijah.

John was also the only disciple who remained at the foot of the cross. When others fled in fear, he stayed.

During a brutal wave of persecution under Roman rule, John was thrown into a massive basin of boiling oil. This was meant to be a certain and excruciating death. But by the will and grace of God, John survived. Miraculously, he was unharmed.

After that, John was exiled to the rocky prison island of Patmos, located in the Aegean Sea off the coast of Greece. Patmos is about 8 miles long and 6 miles wide at its broadest point, a small, barren island by most standards. But it was there, in isolation, that an angel gave John a divine vision. On that island, he wrote the prophetic book of *Revelation*.

Eventually, John was freed and returned to what is now present-day Turkey. He died peacefully of old age, the only one of the twelve apostles not to be martyred.

The book of *Revelation* begins with messages to the seven churches of Asia and then unfolds into a series of prophetic visions, dramatic and symbolic scenes. These all build toward the climactic return of Christ.

By chapter 21, the tone shifts. John sees something entirely new: *"a new heaven and a new earth," "A New Beginning."*

He writes in verse 1, *"there was no longer any sea."* For those of us who live along the California coast, who cherish beach walks and majestic ocean views, this might sound a bit disappointing. But to the ancient Jews, it meant something very different.

In Jewish literature, the sea often symbolized danger, and all that was ominous or threatening. In contrast, rivers and springs were seen as symbols of life and goodness, understandably so, in a dry desert landscape. A stream could mean survival. It represented hope.

Even today, if we look at a satellite image of Israel, we can see the Jordan

River winding its way through the heart of the land, connecting the Sea of Galilee in the north with the Dead Sea in the south. It is a literal lifeline, just as it was in biblical times.

A satellite image of the Jordan river.

So when John says there will be "no more sea," he is not describing the absence of beauty, but the end of fear, danger, and separation. In their place comes the river of life, a spring of eternal peace and renewal.

In verse 2, John writes: "

> I saw the Holy City, the new Jerusalem, coming down out of heaven
> from God, prepared as a bride beautifully dressed for her husband."

This breathtaking vision has inspired countless believers across generations. *"The Holy City,"* is a time-tested hymn that beautifully captures the essence of Revelation 21. Its lyrics echo the majesty of John's vision:

> "Once again the scene was changed, new earth there seemed to be.
> I saw the Holy City beside the tideless sea. The light of God was

on its streets; the gates were open wide. It was the New Jerusalem, that would not pass away."

The image of the *tideless sea* speaks volumes, calm, eternal, undisturbed. No more storms, no more fear. Just light, peace, and belonging.

In verse 3 of Revelation 21, John writes:

"Look! God's dwelling place is now among the people, and He will dwell with them."

What a magnificent prospect, that the Lord our God would dwell *with us*.

And then comes verse 4, one of the most comforting promises in all of Scripture:

"He will wipe every tear from their eyes. There will be no more death, or mourning, or crying, or pain, for the old order of things has passed away."

After so many earlier chapters in Revelation filled with trauma, conflict, judgment, and darkness, after Death and Infernos are cast away, this moment breaks through like the morning light after a long, violent storm. Everything... has become new.

Could it be like that in our own lives? After all the disappointments, closing down a business, heartbreaks, conflicts, trauma and suffering, a time when peace finally takes hold. When the tears dry, the burden lifts, and we find ourselves on the other side of the valley.

He goes on to say in verse 6:

"To the thirsty I will give water as a gift from the spring of the water of life."

After all we go through, our struggles, disappointments, heartbreaks, are we thirsty? Thirsty for peace? Thirsty for comfort? Thirsty for healing?

Are we ready to drink from the spring of the water of life, the spring that offers the healing power of Jesus Christ?

These verses from Revelation 21 have been a cornerstone in eulogies and memorial messages I've given over the years. And time after time, based on the heartfelt responses from friends and family, these words bring comfort. They are soothing and reassuring to loved ones walking through grief.

Because when someone is facing pain, or enduring the final chapters of life, the promise of *"no more mourning, no more crying, no more pain"* is more than poetic, it's consoling, it's calming and it's uplifting. It speaks directly to the ache in our souls and offers something no medicine or philosophy can, and that is path beyond this life.

The book of *Revelation* is not just a prophecy, it is a message of hope, a divine road map pointing us to *A New Beginning*. Are you going through trials right now? Have you been knocked down, feeling lost, discouraged, or even abandoned? Do you feel like the weight of this world has drained your strength and dimmed your light?

Are you ready for *A New Beginning?* You may ask, *"What do I need to do?"* The answer is simple. Open your heart to Jesus. Say this prayer, wherever you are:

"Jesus, come into my heart. I accept You as my Lord and Savior, and I put my trust in You."

Let Him quench your thirsty soul with the water of life.

Let Him guide you, through the narrow gate, down the road that leads to peace, to promise, and to purpose.

With Jesus as your Lord and Savior, you can walk with confidence toward *The New Jerusalem*, the *New Heaven*, the *Kingdom of God*.

And he will give us…A New Beginning.

CHAPTER 26

GUIDING PRINCIPLES

We are what we repeatedly do. Excellence is not a singular act. Excellence is an art won by training and habituation.

ARISTOTLE

M any companies have a mission and vision statement, along with a set of core values. Often, I've noticed, these statements are posted on a company's website or splattered across the wall in the foyer of their headquarters. Yet, when you interact with the people working there, you can barely detect those lofty words reflected in their daily actions.

Don't get me wrong. I'm not suggesting that Sun Valley's approach was necessarily better or more persuasive. What I am saying is that we went through great lengths to truly instill our values and principles into the fabric of the team. Sun Valley's Guiding Principles evolved over time, but by the 1990s, we had refined them into a set of four simple, foundational core values:

- A commitment to be the best in the industry.

- Provide a clean and safe work environment and treat team members with respect.

- Strong commitment to excellence in customer service.

- A desire to be unconventional and on the cutting edge.

In the summer of 2006, during one of our monthly team leader meetings, we asked everyone in attendance to make a list of all the things Sun Valley stood for and believed in.

After an animated brainstorming session, there was a strong consensus around the company's mission: "To be the best flower grower in the USA." The group also agreed to keep our existing core values in place but to define them more clearly and add a few more that reflected who we had become. By the end of the session, we had developed a list of nine guiding principles.

The tenth principle was one I personally added, as I believe it is essential to keep humility and grace at the forefront, no matter the success one achieves. And so, this new set of ten guiding principles was formally adopted in 2006 and carried forward from that point on:

#1 Be The Best That You Can Be.

#2 Treat Neighbors Like You Want To Be Treated.

#3 Inspire Others And Always Keep Learning.

#4 Treat Team Members With Respect.

#5 Keep Our Workplace Safe And Clean.

#6 Delight And Amaze Customers.

#7 Foster A Team Culture.

#8 Instill Opportunities For All.

#9 Continuously Improve And Innovate.

#10 Always Remain Humble And Gracious.

These Guiding Principles were not just posted on the wall in the office; they became the foundation and the fabric of the Sun Valley culture. They were listed in every monthly Sun Valley newsletter, on the back of our business cards, and on a rotating basis, one of the ten principles was highlighted each day.

At the start of each workday, every team would hold a quick kick-off meeting. We would begin with five minutes of stretching, followed by stating the Guiding Principle of the day, and then reviewing the production numbers from the previous day. If other meetings were held, that day's Guiding Principle was also recited to remind the team in our shared values.

In the later years, I began using the monthly farm meetings as a platform to explain the company's Guiding Principles more deeply, sharing stories and illustrations to bring them to life. These meetings could often be lively and full of cheers, but when it came time for the Guiding Principle story, you could hear a pin drop. The team's attentiveness was unmistakable, and their positive reception gave me a boost of energy. Over time, I came to realize that this connection, linking everyday work with a deeper purpose, was one of the cornerstones of the purpose I had been seeking.

Looking back over the past 40 years, across Arcata, Oxnard, and St. Catherines, I conducted nearly 700 of such farm meetings. The "closing thoughts" portion of the meetings started in 2006, and the Guiding Principle narratives began in 2011. These meetings not only shaped our company culture, but they also helped hone my own public speaking skills. The ease that developed from speaking regularly to large crowds would later serve me well, whether delivering sermons or speaking at industry gatherings.

During the meetings, Marisol Marques, a talented Sun Valley team member would translate the stories to bring them to life in Spanish.

The next section of this book offers an outline of the different stories based on the ten Guiding Principles. The "closing thoughts," was a mix of quotes from presidents, coaches, philosophers, Scripture, and even a few of my own reflections. Each chapter of the book started with a quote that was used as one of the closing thoughts in the meeting. The remainder of the closing thoughts can be found in the appendix section of the book.

BE THE BEST THAT YOU CAN BE

Make each day "your masterpiece." Give 100% effort every day. Because whatever you leave on the table is gone forever and you can't make it up tomorrow.

JOHN WOODEN

How do we apply this principle in our daily lives? Let me share a personal story. When I was growing up, my mom often said, *"It's not important what you end up doing, but whatever you do, do your very best."* I took that advice to heart, and over time, it became my life's mantra.

Our family lived in an old, rebuilt bulb warehouse. Attached to it was a tiny, abandoned greenhouse, little more than a sunroom. That rundown greenhouse became my personal project.

I was determined to get the best possible results from that small space. One day after eating some dates, I planted the pits and soon began growing *Phoenix canariensis*, the Canary Island date palm, as potted plants. When they reached about 16 inches tall, I brought them to school and sold them to classmates and teachers.

The little old greenhouse next to our house

I was an average student at best in high school. But after graduating, I enrolled in horticultural college. The school had a greenhouse with nearly a thousand labeled plants, each identified by genus, species, and cultivar. During my first week, I watched one of the senior students walk through that greenhouse, naming each plant from memory without glancing at a single tag. I was deeply impressed and made a quiet commitment; I was going to do the same.

Within a year, I could walk through that greenhouse and name every plant with ease. During the final exam, I identified every single one without a mistake. That experience became a foundation for the rest of my life. While I may have been an average student in high school, I graduated from horticultural college *cum laude* and as the class valedictorian, not because I was smarter than the other students, but because I was driven by a relentless desire to be the best that I could be. That principle, applied with tenacity and intensity, made the difference. And it still does.

As the years went on, Sun Valley faced mounting pressures, costs kept climbing, while customers pushed back against higher prices. In such an environment, the only way forward was by holding fast to Principle #1: *Be the best we can be.*

THE RELENTLESS PURSUIT OF BETTER

One morning, while having breakfast, I happened to flip through channels and landed on a NASDAQ commercial. Its core message caught my attention: *"Good is the enemy of great."* It immediately reminded me of the book *Good to Great* by Jim Collins, a book I read in 2002, yet one that remains deeply relevant today.

In his research, Collins examined eleven companies that transitioned from being good to great. These included names like Wells Fargo, Nucor Steel, Philip Morris, Walgreens, and Kroger. What set these companies apart? Each began its journey to greatness by confronting the brutal facts of their present reality. They didn't sugarcoat the challenges; they faced them head-on with discipline and honesty.

One of the most powerful concepts from the book is the "Hedgehog Concept": the idea of simplifying a complex world down to a clear, focused understanding of what you can be best at. Collins also emphasized the importance of discipline, not just corporate discipline, but personal and team-wide self-discipline, anchored in a strong commitment to guiding principles.

That message still resonates. So how does this apply to the world of flower farming? Did we settle for good tulips, or strive for *great* tulips? Did we want to grow just good iris and lilies, or aim to produce *the best* flowers that surpass any standard in the market? Did we offer merely good customer service, or seek to *delight* our customers with a great experience? Did we strive for just a good team at Sun Valley, or work every day to be the *best* team in the floral industry?

Collins draws a compelling comparison between Kroger and A&P, the Great Atlantic & Pacific Tea Company. A&P, once the largest supermarket chain in the world with over 16,000 stores in the 1930s, eventually declined to fewer than 300 stores by the time it filed for bankruptcy.

Meanwhile, Kroger, a company Sun Valley was proud to call one of its top five customers, continues to grow and lead. From a humble grocery store founded in Cincinnati in 1883, it has become one of the largest supermarket chains in the world, operating more than 2,600 stores and generating more than $100 billion in annual sales.

The moral of the story is this: you must never rest on your laurels. Always look for ways to improve, to innovate, to grow. Never settle for good. Stay relentlessly committed to being better, doing better, until you are, without question, the best.

JERRY RICE

There's no better example of striving to be the best than Jerry Rice, generally considered the greatest wide receiver of all time. In fact, NFL.com ranked him the greatest player in NFL history.

He's a three-time Super Bowl champion, a Super Bowl MVP, a 13-time Pro Bowl selection, and a member of the NFL Hall of Fame. He holds the all-time NFL records for receptions, receiving yards, and touchdowns, unmatched achievements.

But Rice's path to greatness wasn't smooth. He attended a small high school in Mississippi and, although he played football, he wasn't offered a single NCAA Division I scholarship. He went on to play at tiny Mississippi Valley State University, where NFL scouts largely overlooked him, saying he was too small and too slow for the pros.

And yet, Bill Walsh of the San Francisco 49ers saw something others didn't. He recruited Rice, and the rest is history. So, what was Jerry Rice's secret? What made him the best he could be?

In an interview, Jerry Rice revealed something profound, *"I was so concerned about not being successful that it pushed me to be successful."* All those extra hours in the gym, on the track, and on the practice field weren't just hard work, they were about avoiding failure. He said that before every NFL game, he was *scared*, scared to drop a pass, scared of letting his teammates down.

Geoff Colvin, in the book *Talent is Overrated*, describes Rice's legendary commitment to deliberate practice. He often stayed long after his teammates had gone home. His training on "The Hill," a brutal four-mile climb in Edgewood Park near the 49ers' facility, became the stuff of legend.

When A.J. Jenkins was drafted by the 49ers in the first round in 2012, Rice offered to train with him on that same hill. Jenkins declined. He didn't catch a single pass during his rookie year and was traded after one season, a stark contrast, and a powerful validation of the importance of work ethic.

In a *Huffington Post* interview, Rice summed it up: "*There is no shortcut for hard work, determination, and having that 'don't give up' attitude. I just felt you had to work a little harder. It wasn't going to be handed to you. I wasn't the fastest or the biggest, but I was determined to be the best football player I could be.*"

So, what can we learn from this champion? Three key takeaways from Jerry Rice:

- Put in a *volume* of work.
- Focus on the *areas that matter most* to improve your skill.
- Constantly seek ways to *move the needle forward*, don't just settle into routine.

Keep striving to be the best that you can be.

PYRAMID OF SUCCESS

One of the clearest illustrations of the power of Guiding Principle #1 comes from the late John Wooden, legendary UCLA basketball coach who led his teams to 10 national championships in 12 years. While many know Wooden for his coaching legacy, fewer know he began as a high school English teacher.

Frustrated by the traditional grading system, he felt compelled to create a better way to measure success, one rooted not in comparison with others, but in personal effort and growth. He remembered a piece of advice from his father: "Don't try to be better than someone else but never stop trying to be the best that you can be."

That reflection became the foundation for Wooden's Pyramid of Success, a philosophy built on timeless values. At the very top of the pyramid, he placed what he called *Competitive Greatness*, not about being *the* best, but rather, being *the best that you can be.*

Competitive Greatness, as Wooden defined it, is about rising to the occasion and delivering your best when your best is needed. It's also about lifting up those around you. He encouraged his players to *"make each day your masterpiece,"* to give 100% effort every day, because whatever you leave on the table is lost forever. You can't make it up tomorrow.

Sun Valley had earned a stellar reputation in the flower industry, and that was not by accident. It was the result of a team committed to doing their best every single day. In doing so, they not only pursued excellence, but they helped define it.

TREAT NEIGHBORS LIKE YOU WANT TO BE TREATED

Let brotherly love continue. Do not forget to show
hospitality to strangers. For by so doing, some have
shown hospitality to Angels without knowing it.

HEBREWS 13:2

COURTEOUS AND HOSPITABLE

When I first started at Sun Valley in 1984, the relationship with neighbors and the broader community was strained and, at times, contentious. It became a personal goal of mine to turn that around as quickly as possible. Looking back now, I'm proud of how far we came.

Sun Valley became well known in the community for its generosity, whether for flower donations for local events or other contributions that supported the public good.

Of course, operating a farm of our size so close to a residential area meant the occasional issue was inevitable. What mattered was how we responded. We made it a point to listen carefully to our neighbors' concerns and act swiftly and respectfully to address them. In many cases, those who were once critics became supporters, even champions, of Sun Valley because of the grace and sincerity with which we've handled their concerns.

Here's a thank-you note that speaks volumes:

> Thank you so much for including your business in the Taste of Willow Creek event. It was very interesting to have a tour and see what you are growing. Mostly, I want to tell you how impressed our group was with the employees on the tour. They were extremely courteous, hospitable, and careful. They obviously take great pride in what they do. You are fortunate to have employees who represent your company so well. Thank you again and thank you for the Lilies.

THE GOLDEN RULE

At its core, this principle is about one simple yet powerful premise, and that is *Love your neighbor as yourself.* This kind of love isn't just about affection, it's about *care, compassion, respect,* and *forgiveness.* It's rooted in one of the oldest moral teachings we know, The Golden Rule. The Golden Rule dates back more than 3,500 years to the time of Moses. In *Leviticus 19:18,* we read: "*You must not take revenge nor hold a grudge against any of your people; instead, you must love your neighbor as yourself.*"

Fifteen-hundred years later, Jesus reiterated this, saying that the entire Jewish law could be summed up in two commands: "*Love the Lord your God with all your heart and with all your soul and with all your mind. And love your neighbor as yourself.*"

This principle isn't just philosophy; it's a call to action. It's a way of life. And it applies in both big moments and everyday encounters.

At Sun Valley, we installed a digital speed sign along a public road leading towards the farm as a gentle reminder to team members to drive responsibly and respectfully through the community.

Sun Valley regularly donated flowers for local events and fundraisers, including the Cal Poly float in the world-famous Rose Parade.

On December 20, 2022, a 6.4-magnitude earthquake knocked power out across the North Coast. With our emergency generators humming we opened our doors. We offered fresh, hot coffee and phone charging stations so our neighbors could stay connected. The response was heartwarming; many shared their appreciation for this act of kindness.

Operating a farm of our size so close to a residential area meant occasional issues were inevitable. When those moments arose, I asked to respond to our neighbors with dignity and grace. To that point, a powerful Cherokee parable comes to mind:

> Inside each of us, two wolves are in constant battle, one good, one bad.
>
> The good wolf represents honesty, peace, kindness, empathy, joy, and generosity.
>
> The bad wolf stands for anger, selfishness, arrogance, resentment, and fear.
>
> Which wolf wins?
>
> The one you feed.

This principle is a guiding light, calling us to let that light shine before others, not for recognition, but so that our good works might inspire and uplift those around us.

J.C. PENNY

One day, I came across the inspiring story of James Cash Penney, the founder of what we now know as JC Penney stores. His very first store, opened in

1902, wasn't called JC Penney, it was called *"The Golden Rule Store."* You might wonder why.

JC Penney grew up in poverty. At the age of eight, his parents told him he would need to start buying his own clothes and earning his own money. His father gave him a simple but powerful lesson: *"Life is tough, and success only comes through hard work and long hours. But if you live by the Golden Rule, treating others with fairness and respect, things will turn out all right."*

Guided by this principle, JC Penney began a journey that led to success beyond what he could have imagined. He believed you could build a thriving business while also serving the larger community with integrity, fairness, and mutual respect.

This premise was at the heart of Sun Valley's Guiding Principle #2. Let me share a story of something that illustrates the principle.

At one point we conducted a survey of our land and discovered that years earlier we had planted a row of trees about 20 feet *inside* our property line. We had intended to plant them up to the line. A neighbor had built a shed right up to that tree line. When the neighbor saw the survey, she was upset, concerned that she might have to tear down a shed she had used for over 15 years.

I visited her and spoke with her. Instead of escalating the issue, I suggested we draw up a long-term lease agreement, for $1 a year, so she could continue to use her shed without worry. She was genuinely delighted. A situation that could have turned adversarial instead became an opportunity to build goodwill, and we turned a potential foe into a Sun Valley ally. That's the power of living by the Golden Rule.

SUN VALLEY OPEN HOUSE

At Sun Valley, treating our neighbors the way we would like to be treated was important, especially with the farm being so close to the surrounding community.

One of the most effective ways we found to build trust and connection was simply by opening our doors. Our annual Open Houses proved that over and over again. Starting in 1988 we welcomed thousands of visitors each year, and the feedback we received was overwhelmingly positive. The team members were such gracious hosts. The farm looked clean, organized, and vibrant. But even more meaningful was seeing so many team members warmly engaging with our neighbors and the broader community.

We received many thoughtful "thank-you" notes after the events, and I'd like to share one that captures the spirit of the day:

Dear Sun Valley Farms, I took your Open House tour last Saturday. What an enlightening and interesting experience. Thanks to our guide, Clarence, I learned so much about your operation. Clarence took time to answer my questions and explain processes. Your team was courteous and friendly. Thank you for offering this opportunity to our community.

The team didn't just talk about treating others with respect, they lived it.

INSPIRE OTHERS AND ALWAYS KEEP LEARNING

Keep learning; don't be arrogant by assuming that you know it all;
always assume that you can learn something from someone else.

JACK WELSH

YOUR DEMEANOR IS LIKE A MIRROR

How do we inspire others? It starts with being genuine, by speaking from the heart, and showing passion in everything, you do. Inspiration isn't manufactured; it flows naturally when your words and actions align with what you truly believe.

Think about how we greet others. If someone asks, "How are you today?" and the answer is, "Okay, I guess,", is that inspiring? Now compare that to a cheerful "Great!" or "Couldn't be better!" Radio host and author Dave Ramsey always answers that question with "Better than I deserve." That kind of energy is contagious.

And don't underestimate the power of a smile. Your facial expression is a reflection of your emotional state, but here's the secret: it also works in reverse. Your emotional state often follows your expression. That's why many telemarketing firms ask their reps to smile while talking on the phone. Even though the customer can't see them, the warmth still comes through.

Your demeanor is like a mirror, what you project is what you'll get in return. Simple shifts in how we present ourselves can make a profound difference.

Now, let's touch on another powerful way to inspire, and that is to keep learning. What do successful people have in common? They're lifelong learners. Bill Gates reads 50 books a year. Elon Musk learned to build rockets by reading books. Mark Zuckerberg made it a goal to read a book every two weeks.

You may ask, Lane, what books have you been reading? After my cancer diagnosis, I was on a quest to understand and fight the disease. I read books such as *The China Study*, which argues that many chronic illnesses, such as heart disease, diabetes, cancer, are linked to the food we eat. I also read *Chris Beat Cancer*, which explores the role of diet, lifestyle, and environment in healing. I even read about essaic tea, an old herbal remedy with a history of cancer recovery stories.

Let me ask you a question: What book are you reading right now? If the answer is none, I encourage you to start today. Pick something meaningful. Feed your mind.

Inspire others through how you speak, how you carry yourself, and how you keep growing. Be someone who lifts others up and never stops learning.

MAN'S SEARCH FOR MEANING

When universities or high schools hold their graduation ceremonies, a notable speaker will deliver a commencement address. While these ceremonies mark the end of formal schooling, they also signal a new beginning, the start of a lifelong journey.

Some years ago, the Jenkins Group conducted a study and found that 33% of high school graduates never read another book for the rest of their lives. What a missed opportunity. Books are a gateway to continued growth, wisdom, and discovery. Learning doesn't stop at graduation.

I would like to highlight a book that I believe everyone should read, *Man's*

Search for Meaning by Viktor Frankl. This powerful memoir has been named one of the ten most influential books in America by the Library of Congress Book-of-the-Month Club.

In September 1942, Viktor Frankl, a prominent Jewish psychiatrist and neurologist from Vienna was arrested and sent to a Nazi concentration camp along with his wife and parents. Three years later, his camp was liberated. He survived, but most of his family did not.

Shortly after the war, Frankl wrote *Man's Search for Meaning* based on his experiences in the camps. His central conclusion was profound. The difference between those who survived and those who did not often came down to one thing, he wrote, and that was the presence of meaning in their lives.

It's a sobering yet deeply inspiring read. The key takeaway is this: no matter where we are or what we're going through, the pursuit of meaning, by serving something or someone greater than ourselves, is the true pathway to fulfillment. And in doing so, we inspire those around us.

POTATOES, EGGS AND COFFEE BEANS

A father overheard his daughter complaining about how hard and miserable her life had become. In response, he brought her into the kitchen. He filled three pots with water and placed each on a high flame. Once the water began to boil, he added a potato to the first pot, an egg to the second, and ground coffee beans to the third.

Twenty minutes later, he removed the potato and egg and placed them in separate bowls. He poured the coffee into a cup. Then he turned to his daughter and asked, "What do you see?"

"Potatoes, eggs, and coffee," she replied.

"Look closer," he said. "Touch the potato." She did and found it was soft. He asked her to break the egg. She peeled the shell and discovered a hard-boiled egg. Finally, he asked her to sip the coffee. Its rich aroma brought a smile to her face.

"But what does all this mean?" she asked.

He explained: "Each of these faced the same adversity, boiling water, but each responded differently. The potato went in strong and came out soft and weak. The egg went in soft and came out hardened. But the coffee beans… they changed the water itself. They created something new, something better."

Then he asked: "Which one are you? When adversity knocks, how do you respond? Do you let it break you down, harden your heart, or do you transform the situation?"

This story invites us to some deep reflection. In life, things happen around us, and things happen to us, but the only thing that truly matters is what happens within us.

So how can we apply this to our own lives?

Guiding Principle #3 challenges us to rise above circumstances, not only by persevering, but by being a source of strength, inspiration, and learning. Like the coffee bean, let's change the atmosphere around us for the better. Respond to pressure and adversity with purpose.

Inspire others, not just when things are easy, but especially when things are hard. And never stop learning, because every challenge holds a lesson, and every day offers a chance to grow.

Let's make the most of our lives, even in the face of obstacles that may seem insurmountable. As Johann Gottfried Herder once said:

> "Without inspiration the best powers of the mind remain dormant. There is a fuel in us which needs to be ignited with sparks."

Be that spark.

THE GIFT OF PERSPECTIVE

While driving to the farm one morning and listening to the radio, I heard a story that truly stuck with me.

A professor gave his students a surprise midterm. As he handed out the papers face down, he told them not to turn them over until everyone had one.

When the signal was given, the students flipped their pages, only to find a completely blank sheet with a single black dot in the lower right-hand corner.

The professor told them, "Write about what you see."

After an hour, he collected the papers and began reading them aloud. Each student had written detailed descriptions of the black dot, its shape, its size, its position on the page. Not a single one mentioned the white space, the blank canvas that surrounded it.

The professor paused and then said:

"This test wasn't about the dot. It was about perspective. Yet all of you focused on the small black mark, while overlooking the vast white space filled with potential and beauty."

Isn't that so often how we live our lives?

We tend to focus on the dark spots in our lives, the health issues, financial worries, broken relationships, and disappointments. But the truth is, those are small in comparison to the blessings all around us. Our lives are a gift, given to us by God with love and care. There is so much good to notice and celebrate, like the beauty of nature, the friendships we hold dear, the work we do, and the everyday miracles we so often take for granted.

But the black dots can consume our attention, crowding out gratitude and joy.

Let's shift our focus by taking our eyes off the black dots and intentionally fill the page with all the good things in our lives. Count your blessings and let your heart be full.

Gratitude isn't about ignoring life's challenges. It's about choosing to see the whole picture.

MY FATHER R.I.P.

Take a moment and think: Who in your life has been a source of inspiration? Who taught you life's most important lessons? Who do you strive to emulate? For many of us, the answer is likely our parents, our moms and dads.

I traveled to Holland in June 2013, as my father lay near death. Just three hours after I arrived, he passed away. I can honestly say that my dad was a great inspiration to me. He taught me many things, but most importantly, he taught me the values that truly matter in life.

But the role of inspiring others doesn't end with one generation. As time passes, the responsibility to inspire shifts to us. This is where Guiding Principle #3: Inspire Others and Always Keep Learning, comes into play.

Every one of us can be a source of inspiration. It starts with the words we say, words of encouragement, of honesty and wisdom. But it doesn't end there. Inspiration also comes through our actions, small acts of kindness, the way we carry ourselves and the example we set.

The second part of this principle, always keep learning, is just as vital. Finishing school is not the end of the learning journey. In fact, it's only the beginning. One of the best ways to keep learning is to read regularly. 42% of college graduates never read another book after college. 80% of U.S. families did not buy or read a single book last year.

Do not be part of those statistics. Keep your mind sharp. Read books that challenge and inspire you. Let your curiosity lead you to new insights, it will open doors to personal growth and greatness.

TREAT TEAM MEMBERS WITH RESPECT

Remember not only to say the right thing in the right place, but far more difficult still, to leave unsaid the wrong thing at the tempting moment.

BENJAMIN FRANKLIN

ALL YOU NEED IS LOVE

In 1967, the Beatles released their iconic song "All You Need Is Love." It became an international hit and resonated across cultures. The message was simple yet powerful: All you need is love. Love is all you need. At the heart of this message is timeless ancient wisdom.

Renditions of this principle have echoed throughout human history. Confucius said: "Never impose on others what you would not choose for yourself." Socrates wrote: "Do not do to others that which angers you when they do it to you." Buddha said: "Hurt not others with that which pains yourself." These words were spoken more than 2,500 years ago. The root of this principle also goes back to the Bible, and to Moses, who came down from Mount Horeb with the Ten Commandments.

Treating others with respect is a hallmark of love. And this respect shows up in many ways. It's not just about what we do, but also about what we choose not to do. It starts with our words, how we speak to others, and equally, how we speak about others when they're not around. It's about refraining from gossip, choosing a respectful tone, avoiding profanity or language that tears others down, and instead striving to be constructive.

Respect also invites us to pause and reflect. To look inward. To ask, am I building others up? Am I contributing to a culture of kindness, compassion, and dignity? Love and respect are eternal values. They're like a river of cool, refreshing water on a scorching day in dry and weary land, a river that never runs dry. And they nourish not just our own souls, but also the hearts of those around us.

REAPING WHAT WE SOW

September 30, 2016, was a memorable day at the farm. On that day we harvested our very first (organically grown) quinoa crop. Earlier that year, we had planted 10 acres of quinoa on one of the fallow fields on the farm as an experiment. That was in late May. And, just four months later, we were reaping a harvest, forty times more seed than we originally sowed.

The size of a crop depends not only on how much seed is planted, but also on the care the farmer gives it. The principle is simple and timeless; you reap what you sow. It's the law of reciprocity. But this principle doesn't just apply to farming, it also applies to how we interact with people.

When we treat others with kindness, compassion, and respect, when we take time to listen, to be present, and to respond with care, it's like planting seeds in rich soil. And just like the quinoa, those seeds will return a harvest, many times over.

Matthew wrote: *"Whatever you wish that others would do to you, do also to them."* This is the heart of it. Whether in the field or in our relationships, we are always planting. Be mindful of what kind of seeds you sow, because they will grow.

POWER OF THE TONGUE

Treating team members with respect reflects a core belief that *kindness and respect for one another* must be woven into our daily lives.

So how do we show respect? It begins with how we communicate, with our words and with our body language. Speech, though powered by a small part of the body, the tongue, can have enormous impact. It can build up or tear down. It can help or hurt.

As James 3:5 says, *"The tongue is a small part of the body, but it makes great boasts. Consider what a great forest is set on fire by a small spark."* The tongue is like a fire. Used carelessly, it can cause damage that lasts a lifetime. That's why we must be intentional and refrain from profanity and disrespectful language. Be mindful of tone, *how* we say things matter just as much as *what* we say. Strive to be constructive, even when under pressure. It's not always easy, especially when workloads are heavy and days are long. But let's remember, the time we have together is finite. Let's make it count.

This principle of respect shows clearly in our daily actions. It's visible when we support one another, when people go out of their way to help, and when kindness is the norm, not the exception.

The most powerful testimony came from outside voices. Time and again, customers, vendors, and visitors remarked on the positive, respectful demeanor of Sun Valley team members. That kind of feedback didn't happen by accident; it reflected a culture grounded in values. This guiding principle is more than words on a page; it's who we were.

KEEP OUR WORKPLACE SAFE AND CLEAN

Cleanliness and order are not matters of instinct;
they are matters of education, and like most great
things, you must cultivate a taste for them.

BRITISH PRIME MINISTER BENJAMIN DISRAELI

ENGINE FAILURE

For nearly 20 years, we visited the Oxnard farm almost weekly, often flying in a small twin-engine Cessna 414. I vividly recall one trip after a full day touring the farm. About 20 minutes into the return flight, the plane was climbing rapidly to clear the Topa-Topa Mountains north of Ventura. We had reached an altitude of 12,000 feet when one of the engines began sputtering and running rough. Suddenly, the cabin pressure dropped to match the outside atmosphere, a thin and uncomfortable 12,000-foot elevation. Red lights flashed on the dashboard. Alarming beeps echoed through the plane. And then, one of the engines stopped completely.

The pilot turned to us and calmly said, "Folks, we have a little problem. We need to make an emergency landing at the nearest airport in Santa Barbara."

As we approached the airport ten minutes later, two fire trucks with flashing lights waited alongside the runway. The pilot skillfully landed the plane on one engine. Relief and joy swept over us as we touched down safely.

Looking back, it was a close call that could have ended very differently. According to statistics, 57% of plane crashes are due to pilot error. But in this case, we had an experienced pilot, a flight instructor, no less, who had practiced single-engine landings many times. To him, it was routine, because safety was his mindset. Every flight begins with a checklist. No matter how often he'd flown a route, he never cut corners.

Safety was a mindset at the Sun Valley as well. In fact, the safety record kept improving steadily over the years. That was a remarkable achievement. But just like flying a plane, it was not coincidence, it was the result of discipline, preparation, and a shared commitment from every team member.

Just like that pilot who landed safely in a moment of crisis, our team shone when committing to the fundamentals, by being alert, prepared, and always striving to do better.

BROKEN WINDOWS THEORY

In the late 1980s, New York City was plagued by crime, murders, burglaries, drug deals, and car thefts. In 1992, *The New York Times* described the city's bus terminal as "a grim gauntlet for passengers dodging beggars, drunks, thieves, and drug addicts."

The Citizens Crime Commission of New York City published a study revealing widespread fear of theft and assault downtown. Subway ridership plummeted as people feared attacks by gangs or mentally unstable individuals. But then, in the 1990s, something remarkable happened, New York's crime rate dropped at an unprecedented pace.

UC Berkeley law professor Franklin Zimring called it "one of the most remarkable stories in the history of urban crime." While crime declined in other cities as well, none experienced a turnaround as dramatic as New York's. So, what changed?

The answer lies in a concept called the "Broken Windows Theory," which was developed by James Q. Wilson and George Kelling. They hypothesized that ignoring broken windows in both occupied and vacant buildings eventually leads to higher crime rates. If the windows aren't repaired, vandals are likely to break more. Eventually, they may even break in. Or picture a street where a more and more litter appears; soon, people begin dumping entire bags of garbage. Eventually, crime follows.

New York officials took this theory seriously. They launched a program to clean up subway graffiti, restore public spaces, and crack down on minor offenses. The results were extraordinary.

How did this apply to Sun Valley and Guiding Principle #5: "Keep our workplace safe and clean."

A clean, tidy, well-organized work environment is the perfect antidote to the Broken Window effect. Cleanliness sets a tone. It tells every team member, every visitor, every supplier, and every customer that we care, care for our company, care for our shared spaces, and care for one another's safety and well-being.

CLEANLINESS

This guiding principle highlights two deeply connected elements of Sun Valley's daily work: cleanliness and safety. Let me illustrate how these two are intertwined with a few everyday scenarios:

Imagine you're eating at a restaurant, but the restrooms are filthy and clearly neglected. How would you feel about the cleanliness of the kitchen or the food you're about to eat?

Or picture a doctor's examination room with stained walls and a foul odor lingering in the air. Would you feel comfortable having a medical procedure done there?

Or you're boarding a flight and notice the pilot exiting the airport lounge, reeking of alcohol. Would you still get on that plane, or would you quickly turn around and try to catch the next flight?

These may seem like extreme examples, but they powerfully underscore that clean surroundings and clean behavior directly impact safety and performance. Whether in a restaurant, a clinic, a cockpit, or on a farm.

In fact, it's well documented that flower vase life is closely tied to sanitary conditions during harvest and post-harvest handling. Just as food safety and medical hygiene matter in their respective fields, cleanliness in flower production is essential to quality and longevity.

Now think about this. If we were to have added up all the rolling equipment around the Sun Valley farm—forklifts, Tenco's, dump trucks, bicycles, pickup trucks, and golf carts—the total would be surprisingly high. And each one has an operator. Just like the pilot of a plane, those operators carry responsibility for their safety and for those around them.

That's why properly trained, conscientious equipment operators are critical to maintaining a safe work environment. It's no accident that Sun Valley's safety record was excellent, it was the result of the care and commitment of our team.

DELIGHT AND AMAZE CUSTOMERS

The goal as a company is to have customer service that is not just the best, but legendary.

SAM WALTON

LIFEBLOOD OF A COMPANY

Just as the human body cannot function without blood, a business cannot exist without customers. They are the lifeblood. Without them, a business will cease to exist.

We used to refer to this guiding principle as "customer satisfaction." But in a competitive environment, satisfying customers simply isn't enough because that's what most competitors do as well. To truly excel, we must *delight* and *amaze* our customers. This not only sets us apart, but it also justifies the prices required to operate a sustainable business in California.

The Sun Valley team made great strides in living out this principle. Let me share a few examples:

After a long pause due to COVID, we participated in several industry events in the fall of 2022. It was refreshing to reconnect with our customers in person. A common theme in these conversations was how well recognized the *Sun Valley brand* was for its outstanding quality and service. A wholesaler in Miami shared that Sun Valley is "like the Pepsi Cola of the flower business:" his customers always know what to expect when they buy from us.

During the open house in 2022, the team from *The Bouqs Company* visited the farm. Their new CEO had only been on the job for a week. A few hours after their visit, we received this note from her:

> "I couldn't have asked for a better end to my first week at The Bouqs! Thank you for your generous hospitality and including us in the farm visit. I know how highly our team values your partnership and it's easy to see why. I look forward to continued success with you and hope to see you again soon."

Now that is the epitome of *delighting and amazing* customers. Giving them more than they expect; handling their flowers with exceptional care through picking, sleeving, and packing; and occasionally adding a premium variety to their mix. Those details make all the difference. These are the touches that build relationships that are hard to undo and keep competitors outside the door.

The customer is number one. By delighting and amazing them, a team secures its future, together.

GIVING CUSTOMERS MORE THAN THEY EXPECT

A business must be attractive to its customers, because if customers don't feel welcomed, served, and valued, they won't come back.

Let me illustrate this with an experience of some years ago. I needed a few things for the house and yard. I didn't feel like driving all the way to Eureka, so I decided to make a quick stop at the Kmart in McKinleyville, only a few miles away. I hadn't been there in a while.

When I walked in, I saw a group of employees lingering around the cash register, not actively helping customers, just hanging out. As I made my way through the store, I realized the garden section had been permanently shut down, and the electronics area was a shadow of what it used to be. I needed help finding a few items, but there wasn't a single employee in sight. In the end, I found only one of the things I had come in for. Frankly, it was an unpleasant experience. There was a strange atmosphere in the store, it gave me the willies. I never went back.

Now, let me share a positive contrast. The *Country Store* in Arcata, a local breakfast and lunch spot, isn't known for being cheap, yet it's always full of customers. One day, I walked in, and the line was almost out the door. I filled out my sandwich order sheet, and by the time I got to the counter to hand in the order sheet and pay, the cook had already made my sandwich based on what I usually order.

Now that's what I call delighting and amazing a customer. Even though the sandwiches cost a little more, you had better believe I've been back.

In the case of Sun Valley, we gave customers more than they expected or asked for. We provided flowers and services that showed we truly cared. Those things make the difference. They build trust, loyalty, and lasting relationships. That's how you create *customers for life*.

FOUR LEVELS OF CUSTOMER SATISFACTION

Exceeding Expectations by Delighting and Amazing Your Customers. Why is this so important? The answer is simple: the customer signs your paycheck. When you put customers first, they'll stick with you. As Marshall Field famously said, *"Right or wrong, the customer is always right."*

There are four levels of customer satisfaction, and understanding these levels can help guide how you interact with and serve your customers:

1. Meet Expectations. At this basic level, the relationship is functional,

but not secure. The moment a competitor offers a better price or product, that customer is likely gone.

2. Exceed Expectations. This next level improves the chance of a longer relationship, but it's still not guaranteed. If someone else surpasses your offering, that customer may still leave.

3. Delight. When you delight a customer, they begin to look beyond just price. The relationship strengthens.

4. Amaze. When you *amaze* a customer, consistently, they become loyal for life. They stop looking elsewhere.

From my own experience, no matter what challenges come a business' way, the one thing that cuts deepest is when a customer is disappointed or unhappy. That stings. It hits right at the heart. But on the other hand, when a customer is pleased, when you hear their gratitude and excitement, that's like sunshine breaking through the clouds. It lifts you up and energizes you.

At Sun Valley we regularly received positive feedback from customers. One of our top-five customers, HEB, visited both the Arcata and Oxnard farms. They couldn't stop talking about the quality of our product and how much they valued their relationship with Sun Valley.

Feedback like that is what inspired us, and it didn't happen by accident. It was a direct result of the care, commitment, and dedication of the Sun Valley team.

Keep delighting. Keep amazing. Keep earning those lifelong relationships, one customer at a time.

FOSTER A TEAM CULTURE

*Individual commitment to a group effort - that is what makes a
team work, a company work, a society work, a civilization work.*

VINCE LOMBARDI

BEST PLAYER VS. BEST TEAM

In 2014, the world was glued to the television as 32 teams competed for the IFA World Cup. The U.S., Mexico, and Holland all performed well, but in the end it was Argentina and Germany that advanced to the final.

Lionel Messi, the star of the Argentina team and the top-ranked player in the world, dazzled fans with his unmatched skill, quickness, and versatility. Watching him glide past defenders, it often seemed as if the ball was glued to his feet. Yet, for all of Messi's extraordinary talent, it wasn't enough. When the final whistle blew, Germany had won, not because of a single standout player, but because they played better *as a team.*

That's the key takeaway; the best player doesn't always make the best team. Which brings us to *Guiding Principle #7*, and why it matters so much, not just in sports, but why it mattered at Sun Valley. What's more powerful: a few outstanding superstars, or a team that works in harmony? The Sun Valley team was built on teamwork. Let me illustrate this with a real-life example from our day-to-day operations:

Optimal soil preparation sets up the planting crew for success. Proper sterilization of soil and clean crates make planting smoother. Accurate planting density and depth lead to a more uniform crop, which benefits the pickers. Pickers placing flowers correctly in the crates with the right quantity and at the right stage make it easier for the bunching crew to do their job efficiently. Bunchers who ensure accurate stem counts, quality, and correct UPC tags enable the packing crew to work seamlessly. Finally, boxes packed in the correct sequence help the shipping crew hit their deadlines, ensuring our product makes it on time to needed truck connections.

Every role matters. Every step is connected. And everyone's contribution counts. The efforts of the Sun Valley team didn't go unnoticed. I'm deeply grateful for their dedication, their teamwork, and the spirit they brought to this company every day.

Guiding Principle #7 was about reinforcing that spirit. In the "world championship" of flower farming, we aimed to outshine the competition, not by relying on a single star, but by being the strongest *team* in the industry.

NO PRIMA DONNAS

Strong teams win—in life, in business, and in sports. Let me illustrate this with an example. I've been a 49ers fan for many years, and in January of 2020, Tony and I were blessed to attend a playoff game in person. What an experience! The energy in the stadium, the intensity on the field, it was electric. And what made it even better? The 49ers dominated. They played like champions.

What was behind their success that season? Quite simply, they played as a team. I know that sounds like a cliché, but in this case, it's absolutely true. There were no prima donnas. No self-absorbed superstars. These players were focused on *one thing*: winning together.

Take running back Raheem Mostert, for example. He had been cut by six other NFL teams. In his first two years in the league, he never even recorded a single carry. But during that playoff game? He rushed for 220 yards and scored four touchdowns. How? Because the rest of the team, receivers, linemen, tight ends, stepped up, blocked hard, opened lanes, and made those touchdowns possible.

That's teamwork. And what did teamwork mean for the Sun Valley team? Like the 49ers, we worked together as ONE team. No superstars, no prima donnas, no favorites. Just one mission, one shared purpose, to be the best flower company in the USA.

TOTAL SOCCER

On March 24, 2016, the world lost one of soccer's greatest legends. Johan Cruyff passed away at age 68. Born in Amsterdam, he rose to global prominence playing for Ajax and FC Barcelona, later coaching both teams. But his legacy wasn't just about trophies, it was about *transformation.*

Cruyff revolutionized the game with a style known as "Total Soccer," a fluid system where any player could switch positions when the opportunity arose, and teammates would seamlessly fill the gap. It was dynamic and unselfish. And above all, it was *team oriented.*

Soccer journalist Graham Hunter, in his 2011 book *"Barça: The Making of the Greatest Team in the World,"* described Cruyff as *"pound for pound, the most important man in the history of soccer."* Think about that: *the making of the greatest team in the world.* That's something to strive for.

And it brings it directly to Guiding Principle #7: Foster a team culture. What made the Sun Valley team great? It was not just skill or dedication, it was an *unwavering drive to succeed,* no matter the challenge. Like Total Soccer, we stepped in for each other when the moment called for it. We covered for one another. We moved as one. Here are just a few examples that showed this in action:

1. A warehouse team leader *volunteered* to go to Oxnard for the Valentine's Day cross-dock, stepping up without hesitation.

2. The Oriental lily picking team pitched in to plant Royal lilies in the hoophouses.

3. During the holidays, leaders, assistants, equipment operators, planters, and crate dumpers, all rolled up their sleeves to help with *night shift packing* and *tulip bunching*.

4. Our mechanics worked *tirelessly*, going above and beyond to keep production flowing.

5. Planting crews paused their own schedules to help other teams during peak days.

6. The Oriental and iris teams picked tulips early in the morning during peak days to help ease the bottleneck.

This is what great teams do. They adapt. They support. They rally together. I saw this many times from the team at Sun Valley. Their commitment, their willingness to step in and step up, reflected the very spirit of what made Johan Cruyff a legend.

INSTILL OPPORTUNITIES FOR ALL

Life is a gift, and it offers us the privilege, opportunity, and responsibility to give something back by becoming more.

TONY ROBBINS

OPPORTUNITIES GALORE

This guiding principle was embedded in the very fabric of Sun Valley's culture, grounded in a fundamental belief: *when team members are given opportunities, they will step up to the plate.* They will grow, mentally, professionally, and financially.

At its core, this principle is about creating an environment where people can rise. It's about helping each person chart their own path forward. It is, in many ways, the epitome of living the American dream. Providing opportunities to every team member was a cornerstone of the Sun Valley philosophy. We took pride in promoting from within, nurturing our own talent, recognizing potential, and elevating leaders who understood our values because they had lived them from day one.

There were so many examples of this journey in action:

- Fernando started in January 1999, washing buckets. He moved up and played a pivotal role in HR, overseeing safety and recruitment.

- Tim first joined Sun Valley as an intern in 1997 while attending College of the Redwoods. His very first assignment? Helping build the Cravo Greenhouse. From there, he went on to serve as Arcata's production manager for nearly 25 years.

- Nick joined Sun Valley in July 1994 with Dennis' lily planting crew, later moving to R&M for a grow-light installation project. Over the years, he became a trusted and respected team leader, serving the company for several decades.

- Dennis began at Sun Valley in August 1987, fresh out of high school. From his early days on the Oriental crew, to leading the Asiatic planting team, he went on to manage our bulb warehouse, a role he held for nearly 30 years

- Marylou, one of our longest-serving team members, began in 1979 as an iris picker. Seven years later, she stepped into HR, and since 1988 she faithfully served as our personnel manager.

There are two sides to this principle. First, the company must create and sustain a culture of opportunity. But just as important, everyone must be on the lookout for those moments when talents can shine. I was convinced that among the incredible Sun Valley team were skills, strengths, and hidden gifts that weren't yet visible to others.

As Benjamin Disraeli once said: *"One secret of success in life is for a man to be ready for his opportunity when it comes."*

The stories of those who rose through the ranks served as a powerful reminder, that opportunities were real. This principle taught everyone to be aware to be ready. And most importantly, to use one's talents, and use them well. Strive every day to be the very best version of yourself.

That's how we grow, as individuals, and as a team.

ACCEPTING THINGS AS THEY COME

At birth, we come into this world with the abilities provided by our Heavenly Father, the ability to walk, to talk, to learn, to grow, to earn, and ultimately, to give back. As we journey through life, we encounter many forks in the road, and at each one, we must choose which path to take. Some of those choices will serve us well. Others may lead to struggle.

We can spend time second-guessing the past, but that's a futile exercise. Life is not defined by the missteps we make, or even by the setbacks we face. What truly shapes our lives is our response, our dedication, our work ethic, our discipline, and above all, our determination to never give up.

Guiding Principle #8 is Instill Opportunities for All. At first glance, this may seem one-dimensional, a principle that simply calls upon the company to provide opportunities. And yes, it is absolutely the company's responsibility to create an environment where opportunities are real, visible, and accessible. But that is only half the story.

This principle is two-dimensional. It requires the active participation of every team member. Opportunities can't just be handed out like tools on a bench, they must be recognized, seized, and used with purpose. Sometimes, those opportunities aren't obvious. They may be subtle and hidden, like diamonds in the rough. It takes determination, courage, and a willingness to dig deeper to see them for what they are.

The road to success is paved with stories of people who gave up too early, thinking they had done all they could, only to walk away discouraged. But the ultimate champions? They keep going. They press on. They accept challenges without complaint. They listen, they learn, and one day, they arrive.

CONTINUOUSLY IMPROVE AND INNOVATE

For time and the World do not stand still. Change is
the law of life. And those who look only to the past
or the present are certain to miss the future.

JOHN F. KENNEDY

INNOVATION SPIRIT

What do these companies have in common? Montgomery Ward, RCA, Bethlehem Steel, Pan Am Airlines, MCI, Compaq Computer, Circuit City, Woolworth.

At one point in the past 50 years, each of these companies has been a leader in its industry. Today, most are gone, out of business. Why? Because their competitors did a better job at improving and innovating.

Jack Welch, the legendary CEO of General Electric, once said: "*If the rate of change on the outside exceeds the rate of change on the inside, the end is near.*"

Now consider Apple. It started in a garage in 1976, founded by Steve Jobs and Steve Wozniak. For more than 20 years, Apple focused on personal computers, such as the Apple II and the Macintosh. But by the 1990s, sales were faltering. Revenues dropped from $11 billion in 1995 to $5.2 billion in 2002. The company was losing money and losing ground to giants such as IBM, HP, and Dell. Had Apple continued down the same path, it may not have survived.

But then came the game-changer. In 2001, Apple introduced the iPod, and soon after, iTunes, starting a wave of innovation that transformed Apple from a struggling computer company into a global consumer electronics and media powerhouse, with revenues of nearly $400 billion in 2024.

What can we learn from this? Like Apple, Sun Valley was also operating in a highly competitive environment, facing tremendous pressure from lower-cost flower imports from South America. But we were not standing still.

At Sun Valley Guiding Principle #9: Inspire Innovation and Continuous Improvement challenged everyone to look for better ways to do what we do, to adapt and to evolve, to uncover the next breakthrough that will set us apart. For years, our core crops were the "big three," tulips, lilies, and iris. But we diversified, adding crops such as Butterfly Ranunculus.

Then we launched our own hybridizing program for Ilex and Rosehips, and the Lord blessed us with outstanding varieties: Autumn Spirit, Pumpkin Spirit, Winter Spirit, and Gold Spirit. These innovations were not accidents. They were the product of thinking ahead and believing there's a better way forward.

The principle holds for all businesses and even individuals. If you remain sharp, alert, and open to new ideas, you will not just survive but thrive and will stay relevant in the marketplace today and tomorrow.

THE PEYTON MANNING STORY

In October 2018, we attended the PMA Fresh Summit in Orlando, Florida. This premier event brought together 25,000 professionals from the global produce and flower industries. Throughout the show, we welcomed many of our key supermarket customers, including Safeway, Trader Joe's, Kroger, Whole Foods, Walmart, Sam's Club, Sprouts, and 1-800-Flowers, who stopped by to connect and see our latest offerings.

The event kicked off with a breakfast keynote by legendary NFL quarterback Peyton Manning. He shared his personal journey, weaving lessons from his well-known football career into nuggets of wisdom applicable to all walks of life, including our own pursuit of excellence.

Manning emphasized that the little things matter. He recounted how, even as professionals, he and his brother Eli would return to their high school coach to revisit the fundamentals. He encouraged the audience to embrace disruption, especially when things don't go as planned. "Get back to zero," he said, don't dwell on disappointments or failures, but reset, refocus, and move forward.

To illustrate his point, he noted that in his rookie NFL season, he set the record for 28 interceptions, a record that still stands. But instead of being paralyzed by failure, he returned to the basics and leaned into his guiding principles. He reminded the audience that success often comes after setbacks, and it requires the courage to evolve.

"When necessary," he said, "change the strategy without losing the vision. Abandon old routines to get new results. Commit to something inherently uncomfortable." His closing message was powerful: "You never stay the same. You either get better, or you get worse."

These insights resonated deeply with our guiding principle to continuously improve and innovate. Just like in football, Sun Valley operated in a high-stakes, competitive environment, in our case, the global flower market. The only way to thrive was to stay grounded in our purpose and keep getting better.

EVOLUTION VS. REVOLUTION

When was the last time you wrote a letter? Not a thank-you note or birthday card, but an actual letter. One in which you shared a story, described a situation, or laid out your thoughts in detail. It was not that long ago that letters were a central part of daily life. For thousands of years, letters were the primary form of communication over long distance. But in just the past 30 years, that has changed dramatically. First came cell phones and email, then Facebook, Twitter, and texting. What took days or weeks to communicate is now shared in seconds.

Even the companies shaping this communication revolution have changed. Two decades ago, Nokia and Motorola were the giants of the mobile phone world. Today, Apple and Samsung dominate. That's innovation at work, and it happens fast. The message is clear, no one can afford to stand still. If you do, you risk being overtaken and left behind.

I was reminded of this reality during the summer of 2015, when we attended a floral convention in Monterey. The choice of location wasn't just about the scenic beauty, but it was also symbolic. Monterey, along with nearby Watsonville, Salinas, and Half Moon Bay, was once the beating heart of the American flower industry. In the 1980s, it was *the* place to be if you were growing flowers in the U.S.

I remember visiting Watsonville in 1985 to learn from the iris growers in that region. At the time, Sun Valley only grew iris in the spring and a few in summer, but not year-round. Back then, the greater Monterey Bay area produced roughly 80% of the iris grown in the U.S., supported by more than 50 individual growers.

Fast forward thirty years to our 2015 trip when we visited the last remaining iris grower in Watsonville. Just one. The rest were gone. It was a stark reminder that innovation and disruption aren't limited to technology companies. The flower business, too, is subject to powerful and sometimes painful shifts.

Thirty years ago, South America was a small but growing player in the flower market. Today, Colombia, Ecuador, and Costa Rica supply 80% of all flowers sold in the United States. In that same period, rose production in Watsonville declined by 90%.

These are examples of why it's more important than ever for any business to remain sharp, curious, and proactive. Your continued relevance and success will be determined by your willingness to improve, innovate, and adapt, not only to survive, but to lead.

(Note: Sun Valley's drive to continue to improve and innovate was prevalent for many years. After the series of severe financial setbacks described earlier in this book, it became increasingly more difficult for Sun Valley to keep up with the competition, mainly because the capital requirements to stay in the race were unattainable for a company like ours that was caught up in the midst of a debt spiral.)

ALWAYS REMAIN HUMBLE AND GRACIOUS

True humility is not thinking less of yourself,
it is thinking of yourself less.

C.S. LEWIS

HUMILITY

Why is it important to always stay humble and gracious? I cringe when I hear someone boasting. The old saying, *"Pride comes before the fall,"* is more than just a proverb, it has universally been understood for generations. And yet, despite how widely it's known, pride continues to seduce people with its enticing grip.

Let me illustrate this with an example. Growing up, my parents instilled this principle in me repeatedly. When I came to the USA, I was reminded of it vividly as I witnessed the meteoric rise of Melridge, as described in Chapter 5, followed by the hubris of its CEO and the company's eventual collapse. At the time, I was still in my late twenties, just beginning to chart my own path. The experience left a deep impression on me. It confirmed the truth of what my parents had taught me, and I resolved to anchor my life and work in humility, so I would not fall into the same trap.

Webster's Dictionary, along with many others, defines pride in striking terms: An unduly high opinion of oneself, exaggerated self-esteem, and a puffed-up and inflated ego.

What may begin as a justified and reasonable sense of self-respect, acknowledging one's hard work and accomplishments, can quickly erode into arrogance. When that happens, humility gives way to haughtiness.

Scripture warns us clearly and directly:

> "Pride goes before destruction, and a haughty spirit before a fall. Better to be of a humble spirit with the lowly, than to divide the spoil with the proud."(Proverbs 16:18)

> "Before destruction the heart of a man is haughty, and before honor is humility." (Proverbs 18:12)

The world is full of cautionary tales, of companies, kingdoms, movie stars, sports heroes, and marriages brought down by unchecked pride. We see these stories unfold every day on television and social media. Pride doesn't just threaten individuals; it can dismantle entire institutions.

At Sun Valley, we long believed that humility and grace are not just virtues, but they are foundations. Why? Because humility was the cornerstone of how we did business, how we treated each other, and how we lived our lives. Over the years, Sun Valley grew into one of the leading companies in the U.S. flower industry. At one point, nearly 30% of the tulips sold in America came from Sun Valley, and 85% of all iris sold across the country. It was tempting to boast about our accomplishments, but we did not do so.

As Solomon wisely wrote:

> "Let another praise you, and not your own mouth; a stranger, and not your own lips."(Proverbs 27:2)

No matter where you are in life, no matter what success you've achieved, no matter how far a company may go, never lose sight of humility. It's the quality that brings wisdom, builds trust, and allows the light to shine through you.

Let your cup be filled with grace and humility, and you will walk a path that honors both purpose and principle.

WALKING THE HUMBLE PATH

What does this guiding principle really mean? Some of you might be thinking, *"Okay, Lane, you keep talking about being humble, but how do we actually live that out?"* That's a fair question. Being humble isn't easy. It requires intentional effort, self-awareness, and a willingness to grow. Let me offer a few practical ways you can put humility into practice in your daily lives:

1. Listen. The greatest tool in your humility toolbox is something we all have, our ears. God gave us two ears and only one mouth, we ought to use them in that proportion. Listening shifts the focus away from us and places it where it belongs, on others. True humility often starts by simply paying attention.

2. Learn to say, "I don't know." Admitting that we don't have all the answers is not a weakness, it's actually a strength. Pretending to know it all can lead to poor decisions and broken trust. There's great freedom in saying, "I don't know, but I'm willing to find out." Only one is all-knowing, our Heavenly Father.

3. Encourage others. Everyone appreciates a kind word, a pat on the back, or a moment of genuine recognition. Take the time to cheer on the people around you. When you lift others up, you create a culture of encouragement, and that's a reflection of humility in action.

4. Learn to apologize. Sometimes a simple "I'm sorry" can go a long way. When we express empathy and concern for how our actions

may have affected others, we elevate humility from an abstract concept to something that can be deeply felt.

The principle of humility is as old as scripture itself. The Book of Chronicles speaks to the importance of humility more than any other book in the Bible. And throughout the New Testament, humility is presented as a foundational aspect of Christian life and character.

Sun Valley grew immensely over a span of 30 years. It was tempting to feel proud, to share with friends, customers, or even strangers just how large and successful the company had become. And yes, there was a certain joy in seeing how far we had come. But repeatedly I offered this word of caution: be careful not to boast.

Continue to walk the path with humility, listen more, learn always, encouraging others, and owing to your mistakes when needed. Stay on this course, and the light will shine on you.

EPILOGUE

These past 40 years have been incredibly fulfilling. We built a company with a stellar reputation in the American floral industry. At one point, Sun Valley stood as the undisputed leader in domestic flower production. The Sun Valley brand became well known, recognized as the gold standard across many crops. The marketing efforts we undertook were bold, imaginative, and often ahead of their time. Many of those initiatives will live on in the memories of those who were part of them.

But what gives me the deepest sense of gratitude and satisfaction is the impact we made on people, not only within the Sun Valley organization, but across the broader floral industry, both in the United States and abroad. That legacy of people, relationships, and purpose is what I carry with me most.

The pursuit of purpose does not end with the writing of this book. It continues. And to borrow from the words of Erma Bombeck: *"When I stand before God at the end of my life, I would hope that I would not have a single bit of talent left, and could say, 'I used everything you gave me.'"*

I thank the Lord for the many opportunities and second chances He has given me. My hope is that this book has offered not only a glimpse into one man's journey, but also a measure of inspiration, encouraging you in your own pursuit of purpose.

Thank you,
Lane

APPENDIX

CLOSING THOUGHTS BASED
ON GUIDING PRINCIPLE #1:

There is only one reason for doing anything that you set out to do, and that is to do your best. If you don't want to be the best, then there is no reason to go out and trying to accomplish anything.

JOE MONTANA

Winning seems so important, but it actually is irrelevant. Having attempted to give your all is what matters. And we are the only ones who really know the truth about our own capabilities and performance.

Did we do our best at this point in our life? Did we leave all we had to give on the field, in the classroom, at the office or in the trenches? If we did, then we are a success at that stage in our life.

JOHN WOODEN

If you have zest and enthusiasm, you attract zest and enthusiasm. Life does give back in kind.

NORMAN VINCENT PEALE

*Look at a day when you are supremely satisfied at the
end. It was not a day when you sat around.*

MARGARET THATCHER

*I am a great believer in luck, and I find the
harder I work, the more I have of it.*

THOMAS JEFFERSON:

*It is no use saying: "We are doing our best." You
have got to succeed in doing what is necessary.*

WINSTON CHURCHILL

CLOSING THOUGHTS BASED
ON GUIDING PRINCIPLE #2.

I have decided to stick with love; hate is too big a burden to carry.

MARTIN LUTHER KING

*And he answered, "You shall love the Lord your God with all
your heart, and with all your soul, and with all your strength,
and with all your mind; and your neighbor as yourself.*

LUKE 10:27

*If love of neighbor only comes from an obligation to satisfy, it
is a short lived, like melting ice-cream on a hot summer day.*

*But if love of neighbor comes from the heart, from
an innate desire to help others, it is like a rock in
the ocean unwavering even in fiercest storms.*

LDV

*People don't care how much you know until
they know how much you care.*

THEODORE ROOSEVELT

*Peace on earth will come to stay,
when we live Christmas every day.*

HELEN STEINER RICE

*Let brotherly love continue. Do not forget to show
hospitality to strangers. For by so doing, some have
shown hospitality to Angels without knowing it.*

HEBREWS 13:2

*But he has already made it plain how to live, what to do, what
God is looking for in men and women. It is quite simple: Do what
is fair and just to your neighbor. Be compassionate and loyal in
your love. And don't take yourself too seriously, take God seriously.*

MICAH 6:8

*There is a better thing than the observance of
Christmas day and that is, keeping Christmas.*

*Are you willing to believe that love is the strongest thing in the
world – stronger than hate, stronger than evil, stronger than
death – and that the blessed life which began in Bethlehem 2000
years ago is the image and brightness of the Eternal Love?*

*Then we can keep Christmas. And if you can keep
Christmas for ONE day, why not always?*

HENRY VAN DYKE

CLOSING THOUGHTS BASED
ON GUIDING PRINCIPLE #3.

Anyone who stops learning is old, whether at twenty or eighty. Anyone who keeps learning stays young. The greatest thing in life is to keep your mind young.

HENRY FORD

You don't lose. You either win or you learn.

NELSON MANDELA

Knowing is not enough we must apply, willing is not enough we must do.

JOHAN WOLFGANG VON GOETHE

We live in challenging times, affecting our community, our industry and the world at large

Meanwhile 80% of the team in Arcata has less than 9 months of experience. Such a young team will stumble on occasion. There is nothing wrong with that, as long as we learn from it.

Allow any experience positive or negative to be an opportunity for growth. Focus on learning and continue to improve every day.

In the end we will prove to the community, the flower industry, and to the world that our resiliency and drive for excellence can overcome even the most challenging obstacles.

LDV

An arrow can only be shot by pulling it backward. When life is dragging you back with difficulties, it means it's going to launch you into something great. So just focus and keep aiming.

INDIAN PROVERB

Success is how you bounce on the bottom; by perseverance,
study, and internal desire, any man can become great.

GENERAL GEORGE S. PATTON:

The great names in history; be they people, sport teams, or companies,
never started out with the distinction of greatness. Often, they
were shaped by the adversity they endured and mastered.

One can only truly become "Great" if the
circumstances extract the best from us.

The Sun Valley team has had its share of adversity.
Let it be an opportunity to shape us and become
the best flower company in the USA.

LDV

Good actions give strength to ourselves and
inspire good action in others.

PLATO

When you talk, don't say any bad things. But say things that
people need--things that will help other people become stronger.
Then the things you say will help the people who listen to you."

PAUL'S LETTER TO THE BELIEVERS
IN EPHESUS (EPHESIANS 4:29)

CLOSING THOUGHTS BASED
ON GUIDING PRINCIPLE #4.

Love each other with genuine affection and
take delight in honoring each other.

PAUL'S LETTER TO THE ROMANS (ROMANS 12:10)

The best thing to give to your enemy is forgiveness.
To an opponent, tolerance
To your child, a good example,
To a father, deference
To your mother, conduct that will make her proud of you,
To yourself, respect.
To all men, charity.

BENJAMIN FRANKLIN.

Love is the only force capable of transforming an enemy into a friend.

MARTIN LUTHER KING

Remember this: He which sows sparingly will also reap sparingly; he who sows generously will also reap generously.

PAUL'S LETTER TO THE
CORINTHIANS (2CORINTHIANS 9:6)

It is Christmas every time you let God love others through you....Yes, it is Christmas every time you smile at your brother and offer him a hand.

MOTHER TERESA

Getting along with each other, and peace of mind, are the true riches of life.

LDV

An eye can threaten like a loaded and leveled gun, or can insult like hissing or kicking or, in its altered mood, by beams of kindness, it can make the heart dance with joy.

RALPH WALDO EMERSON

CLOSING THOUGHTS BASED
ON GUIDING PRINCIPLE #6.

Satisfaction is a rating. Customer loyalty is a brand.

SHEP HYKEN

We see our customers as invited guests to a party, and we are the hosts. It's our job every day to make every important aspect of the customer experience a little bit better."

JEFF BEZOS.

CLOSING THOUGHTS BASED
ON GUIDING PRINCIPLE #7.

"People who work together will win, whether it be against complex football defenses or the problems of modern society."

VINCE LOMBARDI

Coming together is a beginning, keeping together is progress, working together is success

HENRY FORD

The way a team plays as a whole determines its success. You may have the greatest bunch of individual stars in the world, but if they don't play together, the club won't be worth a dime.

BABE RUTH

Teams that are used to losing may find themselves ahead in a game. But beneath the surface, there's a quiet, nagging feeling, a sense that they don't really belong in the lead. That maybe they're out of place. And more often than not, by the time the final whistle blows, they end up where they've always been, on the losing end.

In contrast, winning teams might trail for most of the game. But they don't panic. They carry a quiet confidence, an unshakable belief that when it matters most, they'll find a way. It's like gravity pulling steel to a magnet. They make the right moves at the right time. Because that's what winners do. They show up when it counts.

LDV

You cannot attain and maintain physical condition unless you are morally and mentally conditioned. And it is impossible to be in moral condition unless you are spiritually conditioned. I always told my players that our team condition depended on two factors: how hard they worked on the floor during practice and how well they behaved between practices.

JOHN WOODEN

CLOSING THOUGHTS BASED
ON GUIDING PRINCIPLE #8.

Be very careful, then, how you live , not as unwise but as wise, making the most of every opportunity.

**PAUL'S LETTER TO THE BELIEVERS
IN EPHESUS (EPHESIANS 5:15)**

Put yourself in a state of mind where you say to yourself, 'Here is an opportunity for me to celebrate like never before, my own power, my own ability to get myself to do whatever is necessary.

MARTIN LUTHER KING

Ask, and it will be given to you.
Seek, and you will find.
Knock, and the door will be opened to you.

JESUS OF NAZARETH

*Don't worry when you are not recognized but
strive to be worthy of recognition.*

*"Character" is like a tree and "reputation" like a shadow.
The shadow is what we think of it; the tree is the real thing.*

ABRAHAM LINCOLN

*A pessimist sees the difficulty in every opportunity; an
optimist sees the opportunity in every difficulty.*

WINSTON CHURCHILL

*Gratitude can transform common days into
thanksgivings, turn routine jobs into joy and
change ordinary opportunities into blessings.*

WILLIAM ARTHUR WARD

CLOSING THOUGHTS BASED
ON GUIDING PRINCIPLE #9.

*Learning and innovation go hand in hand. The
arrogance of success is to think that what you did
yesterday will be sufficient for tomorrow.*

WILLIAM POLLARD

*If you can't turn loose, you never get on with your life and discover
that beyond the dark night is the rising of the sun, otherwise you are
stuck where you are, and the future is simply a repetition of today*

HAROLD SALA

*Build up your weaknesses until they become your strong
points. The best thing I ever learned in life was that
things have to be worked for. A lot of people seem to*

think there is some sort of magic in making a winning
football team. There isn't, but there's plenty of work.

KNUTE ROCKNE

Your time is limited, so don't waste it living someone
else's life. Don't be trapped by dogma, which is living
with the results of other people's thinking.

Don't let the noise of others' opinions drown out your own
inner voice. And most important, have the courage to follow
your heart and intuition, they somehow already know what
you truly want to become. Everything else is secondary.

STEVE JOBS

Continuous effort—not strength or intelligence—
is the key to unlocking our potential.

WINSTON CHURCHILL

Most of us understand that innovation is enormously important.
It is the only insurance against irrelevance.
It is the only guarantee of long-term customer loyalty.
It is the only strategy for outperforming in a dismal economy.

GARY HAMEL, AUTHOR
AND BUSINESS CONSULTANT.

CLOSING THOUGHTS BASED
ON GUIDING PRINCIPLE #10.

The unthankful heart… discovers no mercies; but let the thankful
heart sweep through the day and, as the magnet finds the
iron, so it will find, in every hour, some heavenly blessings!"

HENRY WARD BEECHER

If my people who are called by my name humble themselves, and pray and seek to please me and turn from their wicked ways, then I will hear from heaven and will forgive their sin and heal their land.

2 CHRONICLES 7:14

Finally, all of you, be like minded, be sympathetic, love one another, be compassionate and humble.

PETER'S FIRST LETTER TO BELIEVERS
IN MODERN DAY TURKEY (1PETER3:8)

Wisdom and contentment are like a fresh spring, flowing like an everlasting fountain for those who open their hearts, show humility and are eager to listen.

LDV

Before I was humbled, I was like a stone lying in deep mud, and he who is mighty, came and in his compassion, raised me up and indeed lifted me high up and placed me on the top of the wall. And from there I shout out in gratitude to the Lord for his great favors in this World and forever.

ST. PATRICK

OTHER CLOSING THOUGHTS

After the 2008 immigration disaster, our monthly meetings took on a new purpose, to instill hope, restore confidence, and foster a spirit of resilience in the team as we faced the challenges ahead. Many of the messages shared during these meetings were crafted with that goal in mind. They weren't always tied directly to one of our guiding principles but instead carried an inspirational undertone, designed to uplift, encourage, and remind everyone of our collective strength. From time to time, I also included some of my own reflections, drawn from personal experience, to reinforce those messages.

> *When you get into a tight place and everything goes against you,*
> *it seems you could not hang on a minute longer, never give up*
> *then, for that is just the place and time that the tide will turn.*
>
> **HARRIET BEECHER STOWE**

> *In the middle of every difficulty lies opportunity.*
>
> **ALBERT EINSTEIN**

The spirit of man is more important than mere physical strength.

DWIGHT EISENHOWER

In our journey of life, we will see sunny days,
and we will travel through green pastures.
But inevitably at some point, we will all
encounter that "dark valley."
When hope becomes elusive, it is tempting to
abandon the journey and sit down in despair.
With determination and faith, we shall continue the journey.
The light of the world will shine on those who believe. The
valley will ultimately prove to be beautiful and lush.
Have hope, faith, and an unwavering determination
to succeed and good things will happen.

LDV

Ability is what you're capable of doing. Motivation determines
what you do. Attitude determines how well you do it.

LOU HOLTZ

Everyone is born with a certain potential. You may
never achieve your full potential, but how close you come
depends on how much you want to pay the price.

RED AUERBACH

Work and sacrifice, perseverance, competitive drive,
selflessness, and respect for authority are the price that each
one must pay to achieve any goal that is worthwhile.

VINCE LOMBARDI

As we express gratitude, we must never forget that the highest
appreciation is not to speak the words, but to live by them.

JOHN F KENNEDY

*In war the only defense is offense, and the efficiency of the
offense depends on the warlike souls of those conducting it.*

GEORGE PATTON

*A man can be a great as he wants to be. If you believe
in yourself and have the courage, the determination, the
dedication, the competitive drive, and if you are willing
to sacrifice the little things in life and pay the price for
the things that are worthwhile, it can be done.*

VINCE LOMBARDI

*Nothing can be more hurtful to the organization than
the neglect of discipline. Because discipline, more than
numbers gives one army superiority over another.*

GEORGE WASHINGTON

*It is easy to have discipline and faith in yourself when you
are winning, but if you want to be a winner you must have
faith and discipline even when things don't go your way.
When you are playing from behind, when the odds seem
insurmountable, when the storm clouds are all around you,
He, who accepts life as it comes, learns, gives his all, perseveres, and
has faith, ultimately prevails and emerges as the true winner.*

LDV

*Success rests not only on ability, but upon commitment, loyalty
and pride. In observing great teams and mediocre ones I have
come to the following conclusion: Great teams are bound
together by a shared sacrifice. They fight for one another, not
for applause or headlines, but because they will not let each
other down. That is the true foundation of champions.*

VINCE LOMBARDI

Failure is not fatal, but failure to change might be. Don't measure yourself by what you have accomplished, but by what you should have accomplished with your ability

JOHN WOODEN

How you respond to the challenge in the second half will determine what you become after the game, whether you are a winner or a loser.

LOU HOLTZ

When you are deeply passionate about what you do. When strife to be the best in the world. Not only does your work move toward greatness, but so does your life. For, in the end, it is impossible to have a great life unless it is a meaningful life. And it is very difficult to have a meaningful life without meaningful work. Perhaps, then, you might gain that rare tranquility that comes from knowing that you've had a hand in creating something of intrinsic excellence that makes a contribution. Indeed, you might even gain that deepest of all satisfactions: knowing that your short time here on this earth has been well spent, and that it mattered.

JIM COLLINS

In every battle there comes a time when both sides consider themselves beaten; then he who continues the attack wins.

ULYSSES GRANT

MLK most famous speech was his "I have a dream speech." In closing let me share with you my dream, I have a dream that someday we will be the best flower grower in the USA, return to a stable financial footing and be able to restore the team member benefits that we have been proud of for so many years.

Give freely again to those that need help in our community,
team members treating each other with respect, no
injuries. Be recognized by consumers throughout the
country through continual brand development.
Be the unequivocal gold standard in the flower industry in the USA.

LDV

These are the times that try men's souls. The summer soldier,
in crisis, will shrink from the service of country. He that
stands it now, deserves the love and thanks of man and
woman. What we obtain too cheap, we esteem too lightly.

Tyranny, like hell, is not easily conquered. The harder,
the conflict is, the more glorious the triumph.

THOMAS PAINE

Laziness casts one into a deep sleep, and an idle person will
suffer hunger. Those who work their land will have abundant
food, but those who chase fantasies will have their fill of poverty.

KING SOLOMON (PROVERBS 19:15)

What do we celebrate on this Thanksgiving Holiday? Of course
there is the Thanksgiving meal, football, and fellowship with
family and friends. But also take ample time to reflect.
No matter what troubles we may be facing.
Step back, allow your eyes to be opened and
appreciate the richness of life.
Fill your mind with gratitude.
It will turn what we have into enough and more
Shortcomings into countless blessings,
It will turn anguish into peace and hope,
Confusion into clarity,
Animosity into grace,

Gratitude brings transparency to our past, contentment
for today and confidence for the future.
Happy Thanksgiving,

LDV (PARAPHRASED FROM MELODY BEATTIE)

I have always struggled to achieve excellence. One thing that
cycling has taught me is that if you can achieve something
without a struggle it's not going to be satisfying.

GREG LEMOND

Obstacles are those frightful things you see
when you take your eyes off your goal.

HENRY FORD

For you know that when your faith is tested, your endurance has
a chance to grow. So let it grow, for when your endurance is fully
developed, you will be perfect and completely need nothing.

JAMES 1:3

Good Friday was a significant day in history. Nearly 2000
years ago this was a day of darkness and despair. Yet it was
part of the journey. There could not have been an Easter
Sunday if it weren't for Good Friday first. There couldn't
have been a resurrection if it weren't for the Cross.
No light without darkness.
Folks, every one of us in our own journey will at some
point encounter the dark night of the soul. But here is the
good news; it will not last, as we will find comfort and
hope in the shining light. The light that brings beauty,
peace and love, is like a deep river providing fresh water
quenching our thirst while stranded in the desert.
I wish you all a blessed Happy Easter

LDV

You need to overcome the tug of people against you, as you reach for high goals. I do not fear failure. I only fear the "slowing up" of the engine inside of me, which is pounding, saying, keep going, someone must be on top.

GEORGE S PATTON

ACKNOWLEDGMENTS

First, I want to thank my wife, Kathryn. She patiently listened as I bounced countless ideas off her and worked through draft after draft. Her love, encouragement, and willingness to hear me out made this book possible.

To all the team members who have worked at Sun Valley over the last forty years, this book belongs to you as much as to me. Without your dedication and hard work, the company would never have grown into what it became.

I also want to thank my late partners, Jacob Rooijakkers and Jan van der Wereld. Their wisdom and friendship shaped my journey, and their families continued that tradition by offering me counsel and support along the way.

To my siblings—Teun, Margriet, and Hester—thank you for proofreading the manuscript. And especially to my younger sister, Hester, who gave me honest, thoughtful feedback and pushed me to make it better.

Thanks to Laura Dunn for helping me refine the biblical references, and to Rollin Richmond, Charlie Hall, René van Rems, Barry Gotlieb, Debra Prinzing, J Schwanke, and Jim McCann for their generous endorsements. Your encouragement meant more than I can say.

A heartfelt thank you to Rob Shibata for sharing with me his insights into the history of floriculture in California, along with the treasured book written by his father, Yoshimi Shibata.

Special gratitude goes to Dennis Kouba, my copy editor, who made the book flow better and read more smoothly than I could have imagined.

A big thank you to Steve Kuhn who did an amazing job with the book design. His insights and suggestions where invaluable. He truly made the book what it is today.

And finally, thank you to Karen and Dan Price for your wise counsel, to Kyle Morgan at the Press at Humboldt for your invaluable guidance, and to Amanda Jedlinsky, Editor in Chief of *Floral Management*, for your constructive feedback and encouragement.

ABOUT THE AUTHOR

Lane DeVries is a Dutch-born flower farmer and the founder of Sun Valley Floral Farms, once the largest cut flower producer in the United States. Over four decades, Lane built a business that became known across North America for its quality, innovation, and integrity. His leadership journey has been marked by resilience in the face of trade disruptions, immigration policy shocks, and financial crisis. Lane is also a lay preacher and motivational speaker, sharing stories of faith, perseverance, and purpose drawn from his life in farming and business.

www.ingramcontent.com/pod-product-compliance
Lightning Source LLC
Chambersburg PA
CBHW021219130626
46554CB00004B/1274